CU00709137

This wise, practically grounded book offers the authors' rich understanding of theory and experience of adolescent behaviour to parents and carers who are managing relationships with young people. Their wisdom shines through case studies, discussions, practical questions and comments that will prove a boon to every parent and carer.

Judge Edwin Cameron, Constitutional Court

We found this book invaluable. No matter what you do or what you achieve, there is no job as difficult and important as parenting. We have three adolescent children, each of them different, with their own unique talents and challenges. This beautifully written book provided us with powerful insights and advice, through the lens of the calendar months of the school year and the challenges and demands within them.

Lauren and Adrian Gore, CEO of Discovery Holdings

Raising a teenager in our complex society can be both demanding and sometimes utterly frustrating. The authors address many of the issues that parents face in an understanding and insightful way that will make parenting less daunting. This is a book that every parent of an adolescent should read and it is highly recommended.

Professor Graham Hall, Past Rector of the
Johannesburg College of Education

This book should be required reading for all parents of children starting high school. It is written by two highly respected people who are on the frontline in terms of dealing with adolescent issues. The result is a no-holds-barred look at the inner world of adolescence with all its life-changing potential for good or bad. Parents are clearly shown how their approach can help or hinder the task of preparing their teenager for being 'a responsible and well-integrated adult for society'. The case studies vividly capture the tough issues facing our young and offer parents a way through when difficulties arise, as they undoubtedly will. The common sense refrain of the book is: first ask, Whose problem is it: the adolescent's, the parents' or the school's?' We would all be doing the next generation a big favour if we shared the philosophy of parenting that is so meaningfully shared in The Adolescent Storm.

Paul Channon, Headmaster of The Ridge School, Johannesburg, and Chairman of Southern African Heads of Independent Schools Association (2008–2010)

A book dedicated to the challenges of parenting adolescents within the South African context is long overdue. This book is well researched and highly informative but, more importantly, has been written using the authors' wealth of experience in this field as well as an enormous amount of common sense. The Adolescent Storm *will appeal to all parents, educators and clinicians – in fact to anyone who has an interest in the well-being of our youth.*

Dr Peta Lynn Jearey, Family Medicine Practitioner

Parents often feel uncertain about whether the way in which they are trying to steer their children through their lives is the right way. This book will certainly help those parents and in turn the adolescents.

Liz Dooley, Director Family Life Centre, Johannesburg

The parents of adolescents often need more guidance than adolescents themselves. The authors of The Adolescent Storm *are excellent guides. They write about the psychological challenges of adolescence – and the challenges of caring for adolescents – in a way that is vivid, accessible and engaging. There is a wealth of wisdom and experience in this book, conveyed in down-to-earth language that every parent will understand. If I was a teenager again, this is a book I would want my parents and teachers to read!*

Professor Gavin Ivey, Clinical Psychologist and Coordinator of
the PhD Psychology Programme,
University of the Witwatersrand

THE ADOLESCENT STORM

A HANDBOOK FOR PARENTS

Dr Helen Dooley
and
Meg Fargher

PENGUIN BOOKS

PENGUIN BOOKS

Published by the Penguin Group
Penguin Books (South Africa) (Pty) Ltd, 24 Sturdee Avenue, Rosebank, Johannesburg 2196, South Africa
Penguin Group (USA) Inc, 375 Hudson Street, New York, New York 10014, USA
Penguin Group (Canada), 90 Eglinton Avenue East, Suite 700, Toronto, Ontario, Canada M4P 2Y3 (a division of Pearson Penguin Canada Inc)
Penguin Books Ltd, 80 Strand, London WC2R 0RL, England
Penguin Ireland, 25 St Stephen's Green, Dublin 2, Ireland (a division of Penguin Books Ltd)
Penguin Group (Australia), 250 Camberwell Road, Camberwell, Victoria 3124, Australia (a division of Pearson Australia Group Pty Ltd)
Penguin Books India Pvt Ltd, 11 Community Centre, Panchsheel Park, New Delhi – 110 017, India
Penguin Group (NZ), 67 Apollo Drive, Mairangi Bay, Auckland 1310, New Zealand (a division of Pearson New Zealand Ltd)

Penguin Books (South Africa) (Pty) Ltd, Registered Offices:
24 Sturdee Avenue, Rosebank, Johannesburg 2196, South Africa

www.penguinbooks.co.za

First published by Penguin Books (South Africa) (Pty) Ltd 2010

Copyright © Helen Dooley and Meg Fargher 2010

All rights reserved
The moral rights of the authors have been asserted

ISBN: 978-0-143-02492-7

Typeset by Nix Design in 11/16 pt GoudyOlSt BT
Cover design by Flame Design
Printed and bound by UltraLitho, Johannesburg

Except in the United States of America, this book is sold subject to the condition that it shall not, by way of trade or otherwise, be lent, resold, hired out or otherwise circulated without the publisher's prior consent in any form of binding other than that in which it is published and without a similar condition including this condition being imposed on the subsequent purchaser.

This book is dedicated to the memory of Nikki Irish – our special colleague and friend who was loved by adolescents and parents alike for her gentleness, her loveliness and her empathic listening.

ACKNOWLEDGEMENTS

We owe our thanks to so many special people who have shared part of who they are with us. We thank you all, and especially:

- Our husbands, Rob Breckenridge and Ken Fargher, for their consistent love and encouragement and their belief in our mad pursuits.
- Ken Fargher for his technical support and rescuing of escaping data.
- Ann and Norman Dooley for their energising spirit and belief in the book.
- Julie Green (clinical psychologist) who advised and read the book and who gave valuable input and encouragement.
- Michael and Justine Fargher for their good humour and level-headed comments and advice.
- Louise Grantham for her guidance and warmth and for giving us this wonderful opportunity to share our stories.
- Sue Grant-Marshall for her generosity of spirit and decency.
- Jenny Ketley for her constant support of the book and the process.
- Nonçeba Lydia Mhlozi for always caring and for carrying the dreams of others on her back.
- Catherine Murray, our editor.
- To all the parents and adolescents who enrich our journey and who try so hard to be the best they can be.

CONTENTS

FOREWORD

I used to be an expert on raising teenagers. That was until my eldest daughter freaked me out by showing off her new bikini to four 13-year-old boys at the pool on a recent family holiday. She was nine years old! But in that moment she crossed the line from 'child' to 'preteen'. And I became a parent preparing for adolescence. And no longer an expert.

In the ever-changing world in which we live, parenting an adolescent can be both lonely and scary. We look to older friends and family, hoping that those who travel ahead of us on the parenting journey may have some answers to our unasked questions. Unfortunately, it seems as if answers are in short supply at present. That's why I was thrilled when I heard that Meg and Helen were planning to write a book on adolescence, and especially on parenting and the school experience. I have long admired both of these women. Their years of personal interaction with young people (and their parents) and their professional expertise have equipped them well for the task of writing this book.

I first met Meg when I was invited to speak at the prize-giving at the end of the academic year at St Mary's School in Johannesburg. Meg was the headmistress, halfway through what turned out to be just less than a decade in charge of Johannesburg's oldest girls' school. Not only was she much loved – and respected – by the girls and the staff, but she had the admiration of the parents, too. Helen is an ideal collaborator. As a psychotherapist with a decade's experience of working in a school setting, she has seen the good, the bad and the ugly, and has successfully worked with young people as well as parents.

This book is an interesting mix of theory and practice, with an unusual approach. Using analogies of the seasons and weather through the school year, and case studies taken from their years of experience, Meg and Helen bring clarifying insights to a complex subject. There is something for both sides of the brain, and informed sensitivity that speaks to heart and head in equal measure.

They do not attempt to offer simple formulas – so common in the 'three steps to success' motivational-type books. Parenting an adolescent requires more than platitudes. Simplistic solutions might make us feel secure, with their promises of easily achieved outcomes, yet they will ultimately frustrate us. Life is not that simple. Clichés are not enough. *The Adolescent Storm* acknowledges the complexity of adolescence and parenting, and by using case studies, it provides principles that we as parents must apply as we help our adolescent children grow into adulthood.

As we read these case studies, parents will recognise their own children, and their children's friends. In many cases, parents will also recognise themselves, instantly transported back to their own turbulent teenage years. This is one of the truths of parenting: that we parent out of who we are. Much of our parenting, especially during the adolescent years, is more about who we are than who our children are turning out to be. When your son asks you if he can use your car for the first time, for example, your response is very likely to reflect what happened to you when you asked your parents the same question. If you had a good childhood experience, you will try and repeat it for your son. If you had a negative experience, you will probably overreact and do the exact opposite of what you experienced. Either way, it's more about you than your son, and this can lead to conflict and confusion.

A good parent is a parent who understands the impact of their own adolescence on their attitudes and behaviour. And a great parent knows that their adolescent child has to learn lessons that can only be learnt by experience. The problem, of course, is that experience is something you only get just after you need it. Parents of today seem to be trying to overprotect their children, cocooning them from the very experiences that will shape and form them into independent adults. Maybe it's because many of today's parents grew up in the 1970s and 80s, when suburban children were often left to their own devices by hard-working parents in dual income – and often divorced – homes. It's possible they're overreacting to largely absent parents in their own childhood. Whatever the reason, today's adolescents need parents who will lovingly allow them some space to grow up into adults, and parents who will continue to grow and develop as confident adults themselves.

Children are a gift. As we hold our newborn children in our arms, the gift is immense, almost overwhelming: little bundles of energy and potential – so precious and fragile. As they grow older, they bring us the gift of laughter, and moments of poignant reflection. They also give us grey hairs as they encounter the dangers of the world. Yet, they are still a gift. When, as young children, they mimic us, we sometimes laugh to hear our adult words repeated by innocent mouths. Sometimes we cringe when they mimic our darker sides as well. That, too, can be a gift. I don't think it is an accident that parents tend to be in their forties when their children are adolescents. During this life stage, adults can often feel they have everything sorted out, and that life has fallen into a pattern. Having a teenager in the house is one certain way to ensure you don't get either comfortable or bored. As disturbing as it can sometimes be, it can nevertheless be treated as a gift. The gift, if we choose to accept it, is a reminder that we, as parents, have not yet finished our own development. This book is as much about parents as it is about adolescents. Each of us is on a journey to become a better adult – parents are just a few years ahead on the journey, with some valuable experience to impart.

I have three daughters, Amy (born 1999), Hannah (2001) and Rebecca (2005), and my wife and I are going to be spending the second and third decades of the twenty-first century with teenagers in our house. I am truly grateful to Meg and Helen for this book. It taps into their vast experience and skills, and provides some valuable assistance on the parenting journey. I know I can use all the help I can get. I'm guessing you do, too.

August 2009

Dr Graeme Codrington *is a presenter, author and future trends analyst at TomorrowToday, a global strategy consultancy. From his bases in London and Johannesburg, he assists companies and individuals around the world to anticipate and respond to macro people trends. He is the author of three best-selling books, including* Future-Proof Your Child: Parenting the Wired Generation *(Penguin, 2008).*

ABOUT THE AUTHORS

Dr Helen Dooley holds a PhD from the University of Pretoria and currently consults in private practice in Johannesburg, South Africa. Prior to moving into full-time private practice, Helen was a school psychologist for 10 years. She has been a psychologist for 12 years.

She has a passion for climbing and adventure and has climbed three of the Seven Summits.

Helen is married to Rob and has no children of her own, but has learned a lot through consulting to parents and their children. She has also learned that being 'too good a parent' to her pets has its consequences.

Helen and Meg conduct seminars for parents. Both consult to parents around conflict or difficult parenting issues.

Meg Fargher holds an MA from the University of the Witwatersrand and taught for 15 years before becoming principal for nine years of one of the pre-eminent schools in South Africa. As a mediator and someone who assists in dispute resolution, Meg is keenly aware that sometimes the adolescent never really leaves us. As a consultant, she is involved in interesting educational and business initiatives and she is passionate about South Africa.

Meg is married to Ken, who is an excellent father to their two now grown-up children, but she insists that she made many mistakes in her parenting and wishes she had had the knowledge then that she has now.

PREFACE

An eminent professor of business strategy commented that he felt that many parents, including himself, were overwhelmed at the task ahead of them as they faced the high school journey with their fledgling adolescents. He postulated that schools should insist on parents attending a compulsory 'pre-high school course' before they were allowed to bring their adolescents to school. The idea is a good one, but the logistics are somewhat daunting.

As we witnessed similar scenarios in our respective fields of work, the idea for this book was born. While one of us, as a psychologist, felt that many parents were arriving at therapy unduly concerned by fairly normal displays of adolescence, the other, as a school principal, was considering how to help parents who were trying hard to effectively manage the process of parenting adolescents. We decided to put our experiences with adolescents together to write a book about healthy adolescents and what parents could typically expect from the journey. Rooting our observations in psychological theory, we have written a book that aims to assist parents in understanding what may be happening on their adolescents' thrilling journey towards adulthood.

Ironically, as parents engage in the rewarding and challenging task of effectively parenting their adolescents, it also becomes a time for them to confront and reflect on their own identities. *The Adolescent Storm* encourages them to engage in reflection and reflective parenting.

Adolescents are a special, almost magical force, deeply selfish, mostly honest and constantly changing, growing and developing into new and unique, more complete human beings. In the early stages of adolescence they are so obviously incomplete, but by the end of the process they are remarkable beings filled with possibility – particularly if adults have nurtured them and been interested in the transition from childhood to adulthood. In our fields of work we have had the pleasure of seeing this wonderful, positive growth and we have also witnessed the pain that parents of adolescents can feel – especially when they are interested in and wanting the best for their adolescent.

Through case studies and concomitant explanations, *The Adolescent Storm* aims to help parents realise that they are not alone in their parenting endeavours. They will learn that there are no perfect parents, no perfect teachers and certainly no perfect adolescents. If parents can enjoy the noisy, sometimes chaotic space in which they find themselves with adolescents, the process of parenting, although trying from time to time, can develop into one where a relationship with one's adolescents can become deep, connected and relevant.

The very fact that you are reading this book suggests that you are a deeply interested and caring adult wanting the best for the adolescent or adolescents in your care.

We both live and work in Johannesburg, South Africa, although we have both dealt with adolescents from around the country. The book is South African in that it sets the case studies into the calendar according to the South African school year, which begins in January and ends in December. The year is divided into three or four terms or semesters, with examinations invariably occurring in the middle and at the end of the year. High school begins in Grade 8, when the adolescent turns 13 or 14, and ends in Grade 12, when the adolescent is about 18. Unlike the northern hemisphere, the school year begins in mid-January, which is summer, and ends in early December so that the students can enjoy December festivities and the lovely weather so typical of this wonderful country.

Many, but not all, of the case studies are set in Johannesburg with its temperate climate, which enjoys four distinctive seasons. Typical to Johannesburg are wonderful, short-lived, regular summer thunderstorms and icy but sunny winters. Cape Town, by contrast, has a Mediterranean climate with a winter rainfall.

The metaphor of the seasons is central to *The Adolescent Storm*. Seasons help to make our lives less mundane and predictable and, likewise, adolescence is a remarkable and dramatic season in your child's life journey. Seasons prevent boredom and each season has its own special attributes, joys and pains. Summer is reminiscent of lazy days, but the heat can wilt the best of moods. Autumn is charming and the changing leaves are exquisite and motivating, but we then have to rake up the debris of the beauty and the peace. Winter is cold and often unfriendly and yet the warmth of a fire – the hearth of the home – engages us with those close to us while paradoxically the coldness of the air adds vitality to our day. Spring is redolent with hope and is suggestive of beauty and growth. Just as the seasons have their moments of joy and light, dark and pain, so it is with the stages we have to go through with our teenagers. Seasons pass. It is never winter forever; there is never endless sunshine nor perpetual sublime autumn mellowness. So too adolescence passes and it would be very sad to have missed out on all it has to offer you as a parent.

The Adolescent Storm has a specific structure. The Introduction presents a theoretical background to some of the assumptions made in the book. Bearing in mind that this is not a psychology textbook, the aim of the Introduction is to encourage parents to consider and understand the developmental stage the adolescent is in when they encounter a challenging parenting moment. (If you are averse to theory, skip the section.)

Each chapter represents a month of the year. Each month represents an event or an emotion typical of that time of year. Case studies are presented and then the developmental considerations pertaining to those case studies are outlined. As parents read the case studies, they are encouraged to ask:

- *Is this a parent issue?* (i.e. unresolved adult/parent issues which impact on how the parent feels about what is happening to their adolescent)

- *Is this an adolescent issue?* (i.e. an issue that will provide developmental opportunities for the adolescent and where the parent needs to be the support structure)
- *Is this a school issue?* (i.e. let the school resolve the issue while the parent remains the solid anchor for the adolescent. If the school does not resolve the issue, what options can parents explore to help their child and what motivates that intervention?)

In order to avoid the cumbersome gender of 'he' or 'she' when referring to adolescents as generic and not specifically in a gendered context, we have tried to use the gender-neutral 'they'. When we refer to adolescent development, no distinction is made between the genders.

We hope the book is enjoyable and encouraging, albeit challenging, for parents. We hope you enjoy the magic of adolescence and make the most of the time with your adolescents before they enter the demanding complexities of adulthood.

We have valued the input that adolescents have brought to our lives, for the wonderful lessons they have taught us about ourselves and about life and we salute all parents who bother to engage meaningfully in parenting their children. It is not an easy task, but done consciously and proactively, parents prepare the path for deep and wonderful relationships with their offspring when they enter adulthood.

Introduction

THEORETICAL CONSIDERATIONS

ADOLESCENT DEVELOPMENT

We will be drawing from Winnicott, a British paediatric psychiatrist and psychoanalyst, when thinking about adolescent development. Winnicott is central to the adolescent theory in this book for three reasons. First, Winnicott believed that early developmental issues are reworked in adolescence. The second reason is Winnicott's concept of the 'good enough' environment and the 'good enough' mother or father, which has particular relevance for adolescent development. The 'good enough parent' and the 'good enough environment' is an important concept to think about in parenting. The third reason Winnicott is valuable when considering the parenting of adolescents is that he wrote explicitly about adolescents and their *unique* connection with the social world.

1. EARLY DEVELOPMENTAL ISSUES ARE REWORKED IN ADOLESCENCE

One way of understanding adolescence is to go back to understanding infancy, because the two developments are similar psychologically. Likening infancy to adolescence might seem strange, but it is surprisingly significant that both age groups are striving for independence while simultaneously needing to be dependent. During these specific developmental stages, both infants and adolescents deal intensely with their sexuality and with finding out who they are in relation to their world.

If a parent considers the reactions of children during the 'terrible twos' (typically when parents start introducing demands on toddlers because they are starting to socialise them) the correlation to similar behaviour during adolescence is obvious. In adolescence, it is a time for finding an identity by hitting out against parent-imposed boundaries. At the same time it is important for parents not to collude with their adolescent's reaction to boundary-setting by giving in too easily. Parents have to negotiate and adhere to boundaries in spite of the hitting out against them so that the adolescent can feel safe when they try to test their metaphorical strengths and burgeoning opinions.

The infant explores, identifies and derives pleasure from all parts of its body, in particular its mouth, anus and genitals. During infancy the entire body is pleasurable to the infant; in adolescence, the adolescent's interest in sex becomes heightened. As in infancy, the exploration process is significant because there are rapid physical changes taking place within the adolescent. Excitement and pleasure are experienced as in infancy, but in adolescence this pleasure is compounded by anxiety since adolescents are still discovering what their bodies are capable of doing and feeling. They are delighted and terrified of their new-found sexual energy, while some adolescents wonder if those feelings will ever arrive. The parents' and the schools' boundary-setting role within an enlightened, understanding context becomes vital.

Infants love their family members passionately; almost incestuously. The first people they love are their parents, typically their mother and father, and later their siblings. Usually there is a great deal of care and attention from the parents. By and large this infantile experience of loving will impact on *who* and *how* the infant will love in future adult years. For example, they will look for the same qualities in their first girlfriends or boyfriends and will treat them as they have been taught through observing their parents' relationship. Infants learn how to relate, play and be creative with their first caregiver and this is carried through into their playing and creativity as an adolescent and adult.

Parents may remember the *rapid growth* of their infants in early childhood and the overwhelming anxiety and joy that accompanied this growth. The intensity of emotions and thoughts little children experience can make this a trying time for the new parents as they manage their own emotions in the parent-child, parent-parent relationship. From birth there is a gradual separation from the mother (or caregiver), through which infants learn to be themselves while remaining very dependent on the mother.

A period arrives in human development when children are in their latency age, from about six to nine years. During this time of latency, sexual energy gives way to general learning. Most children in latency seem to enjoy abiding by rules that are black and white, and that make interactions fair and clear. In many ways the time of latency is the calm before the apparent storm of adolescence. But as in adolescence, storms are powerful and beautiful and completely unavoidable. From storms there is growth and development and change. We can do a great deal to mitigate the negative impact of storms and likewise parents can do a great deal to gain the most from the dynamic and powerful adolescent phenomenon.

During adolescence, that final separation from parents which began in infancy is reworked in the process of discovering who they are. In order to accomplish these 'tasks of adolescence', adolescents need to be able to react against a parent. Through the process of reacting against the parent the adolescent gets a sense of what they truly believe. Like the storm, it is a perfectly natural, powerful and unavoidable event. Ironically adolescents usually take on, as their own, the values that parents have established in the earlier years.

By adolescence there is a marked resurgence in sexuality and sexual development. Adolescents' infantile sexuality is reworked to develop into adult sexuality. Indeed, there is a strong interest in the opposite sex and they may be having sexual intercourse, especially if the adolescent has been in a long-term relationship. Adolescents become preoccupied with their own bodies. For example, adolescents, especially girls, can spend hours in front of the mirror admiring or worrying about what they see. Adolescents may masturbate, especially boys, as they learn about the pleasure that their bodies can give them or they may masturbate to release sexual tension. Sexual dreams may become the norm.

Almost every week the parent wakes up to an adolescent who looks and sounds different and this can impact on the parents' perception of themselves and their adolescent. They may well feel as confused as the ever-changing adolescent. For example, the parent may start feeling less powerful, less wise and less appreciated as a separate person. The parents will find that they are possibly debating many more issues than when their adolescent was in the latency phase. This can be a rewarding yet simultaneously frustrating and difficult experience for both the parent and the adolescent.

In adolescence the physical difference between being a man or a woman becomes more obvious. The body becomes capable of reproducing and the concomitant physical changes are important for adolescents. For example, their genital hair grows, their voices change and they are interested in using their bodies to achieve genital pleasure. Boys are prone to developing voracious appetites, which can startle parents and their household food budget! Girls are sometimes confused by how they feel and what they see. Parents are required to come to terms with their adolescent developing into an adult while understanding that on an emotional level the adolescent may not always keep up with the physical and more obvious bodily developments. As a result of the dissonance that adolescents sometimes feel between their emotional and physical selves, parents would do well to understand the confusion that naturally arises in their adolescent. To hold this dissonance in mind, a good question to ask would be: Where is my adolescent at physically and where is my adolescent at emotionally?

The reason we are explaining these links between the emotional and physical sides to the adolescent is that we believe the purpose of parenting is to help the child, now an adolescent, to develop into a *responsible and well-integrated adult for society*. Thus if parents have greater insight into the process of healthy adolescent development, they will understand, enjoy and, if necessary, adjust their parenting to achieve that aim.

2. THE 'GOOD ENOUGH' ENVIRONMENT OR CAREGIVER

A primary position in Winnicott's theory of early development and its relation to later adolescent development is his concept of a 'good enough' environment or mother. This means that when an infant is born, the mother adapts her behaviour to meet the needs of her infant. This accommodation by the mother provides infants with the *illusion* that they own and have created their mother, her breast and her whole body. The mother allows the infant to believe that the infant found and created the mother as a person, as well as his or her world.

According to Winnicott, at birth an infant has no sense of being separate from the mother. The mother (or father, depending on who the main caregiver is) provides the correct light, heat and noises so that baby can be in a calm, quiet state. The environment completely adapts to the needs of the infant. The mother gives everything, so that when the infant wants milk, there is milk, or when the infant needs sleep, the mother will make sure there is a cosy, quiet spot. The mother recognises that the baby cannot cope with all that the environment offers and tries to mitigate and ameliorate unpleasant or uncomfortable situations. She will try to be as present as possible, keeping in mind work commitments, or she will ensure that the environment will work for the baby. The baby therefore is in a position to feel majestic; usually the baby will get immediate gratification and will feel powerful. A contradiction exists because babies cannot have that all-powerful experience unless the parents are providing the safety for them to feel that way.

Gradually and subconsciously the mother begins a process where she allows the world to enter more and more into the infant's space because the baby is ready for it and is now in a position to separate gradually from her and be independent in taking responsibility for some of its needs; for example, allowing the baby to cry a little to be fed before being fed. From these experiences the baby develops a belief in a benign world in which he or she can be creative. Through these experiences babies learn that the world is safe and that they can explore, play and express themselves in it. Infants still have a reliable parent to depend on and will therefore continue to develop their independence. This is described as a 'good enough environment', where the mother provides a space that is safe enough for the baby to be completely dependent but to gradually move towards more independence. It is 'good enough', because we recognise the importance of the baby experiencing an imperfect environment, where the environment will, at times, fail the baby's immediate needs. For example, the baby may have to cry for milk but the environment has not allowed the baby to starve or feel overly anxious. The experience of receiving the milk slightly later than demanded was 'good enough'.

In adolescence, a similar developmental process around separation can be seen where, initially, adolescents require parents to adapt completely to their instant gratification state. (The instant gratification phenomenon is complicated by the advent of mobile technology, which places extraordinary demands on parents to be available at all times to their adolescent, an aspect covered specifically in Chapter 8.) The 'rule-bound', dependent, latent child has gone from their personalities for a while and is replaced by a very often opinionated, semi-independent adolescent. As in infancy, parents are implicitly asked to be ever-adapting and over time to be less accommodating because as this process helped the infant's intense growth spurt, so it will help the adolescent's intense growth spurt.

We see the adolescent's growing independence in the way they dress and their belief that they can do anything. Their behaviour can be quite reckless and dangerous. When adolescents are in what they believe to be a 'safe enough' world, they can try out all different parts of their identities until they feel content to be who they predominantly are. For example, what part is Madonna-like and what part is St Theresa-like? Or for boys, when are they the magnanimous John Smit (the excellent South African rugby captain) and when are they the reckless, invincible cartoon character? Adolescence is a time where they will judge, assess and feel all parts of their identities. Again, as in infancy, a contradiction exists where they can be all powerful only when they have a reliable parent as a back up and support. Parents can often find themselves thinking, 'Just who do these teenagers think they are!'

A good enough experience for children exists when infants and adolescents feel as though they have permission to play. Play is a relaxed space and its function is to help the individual child or adolescent process and rework their experiences. For example, a four year old who dresses up and imagines she is a princess may adore the attention she receives from loved ones and learn something about her need for attention as well as her ability to create magical thoughts. If she pretends to be something negative, she may be reworking difficult experiences and learning about what fear means for her personally.

Latent-age children tend to be more rule bound, so their play may be less creative and more structured, but play remains to work through and understand different experiences.

Adolescents play at being adults and in so doing they enjoy exploring their identity in the safety of knowing that through play they can depend on their parents if they go in the wrong direction. Playing can include lying on their beds, talking to their friends on their mobiles, wearing clothes that express their current identity – much like the four year old did when dipping into the dress-up box to play at being different people.

Playing and dreaming are extremely important to help adolescents develop their identity. Adolescents in play feel supreme because time and space is under their control. Parents should protect this space and tolerate it; particularly because in today's frenetic society adolescents seem to have less and less time to play and dream.

The 'not good enough' environment or caregiver

If parents do not cope with the bombardment caused by adolescence and do not stand up for what they believe in, then the adolescents have to start to put up their own boundaries and their development is impeded or compromised. This leaves them having to be far more adult than they are emotionally able to be. We consider this to be a 'not good enough' environment to help the adolescent develop into a responsible adult. More definitive limits manifest in anxiety behaviour where adolescents can become very rigid, almost parent-like, and they may deny their own teenage needs. One of the consequences is that they may only explore their own sexuality later and by not understanding different parts of themselves earlier they may be promiscuous in adulthood. Or they can move into risk-taking behaviour such as substance abuse, where they rebel against an adult's modality. Adolescents living with parenting that is either too rigid or too boundaryless will not feel safe enough to articulate their true needs. This leads to a compromised sense of self and a false adolescence.

When space for separation and pushing of boundaries for the adolescent is not permitted and rigid parenting is in place, adolescents are unable to develop their own sense of self. If the adolescent has no healthy sense of self, the ability to relate to other individuals is affected and this can result in adolescents being unable to make authentic contact with themselves and with those around them. By denying the adolescent a space to hear their own voice, the parent could pass on a fragmented understanding of how the adolescent should relate to people outside the family. When the adolescent attempts to separate, as they eventually must, they see only an image of their parent and have no capacity to see their true selves. This context of emotional deprivation could result in adolescents who are compliant and immature in development because they defend and protect against what is real within themselves for fear of continued rejection by the parent and society at large. The result is a false identity and unfulfilling and possibly harmful relationships in later life.

Specific developmental issues in adolescence

A way of understanding the particular needs and emotions in an adolescent's developmental transition to adulthood is to see adolescents as having polarised emotions. The first pole reflects their vulnerability and their childhood state of dependence. The opposite pole, their pseudo-maturity, reflects their need to be grown up; a need that protects them from the vulnerable state where they can experience difficulty in revealing emotions more typical of their dependent, childlike state. Pseudo-maturity assists adolescents in their move to adult status. By acting in a pseudo-mature fashion, adolescents are able to disguise what they see as embarrassing vulnerabilities. Adolescents can then be more true to themselves by being more spontaneous in a place that feels less threatening, such as being with their friends. Allowing adolescents to practise being a more confident but nevertheless authentic person helps them move towards becoming a confident, well-integrated adult.

Understanding how your adolescent communicates this persona may assist you as a parent in understanding interactions with your teenager. Adolescents, however, do not always want to be fully understood by adults. As adults we need to hold this dilemma in mind when we communicate with adolescents and allow ourselves to be confused about them while still offering 'good enough' parenting. Adolescents do not always want to be understood because this gives them space to develop who they are, what they think and what they believe. By being confused and engaging in some conflict, the parent can help the adolescent have space to practise holding on to what they think they believe.

Parents would do well to give adolescents the space to dream and fantasise, while being emotionally involved and interested in their adolescents. Giving adolescents space to explore their sexuality provides them with an invaluable tool because daydreaming can help them to separate from the parent, and feel better about themselves in terms of their worth and identity. For example, talking privately on the phone to their girlfriend or boyfriend is a form of loving and sexual dreaming. Space to dream affords adolescents the opportunity to think about their thinking. Often they realise that perhaps their parents are not all bad and subsequently they learn to value and take on some of their parents' thinking as their own.

Parents need to be present and involved with their adolescents, not so much on a basic, practical level as was the case when the child was an infant, but rather on a greater and more profound emotional level. Engaging meaningfully with your adolescent is vital for their healthy emotional and social development. In 'good enough' environments, there is space to talk about feeling let down. For example, your adolescent should feel safe enough to express that the parent may be 'getting it wrong', whether this is the case or not.

Characteristic adolescent developments that confront parents

Everybody, be they adolescent or adult, experiences some sort of anxiety from time to time and in order to cope with these anxieties we all tend to develop defences. Some defences are immature and unhealthy, for example denial or seeing things in only black and white, which can become an unhealthy defence because it is narrow, dead-end thinking (black-and-white thinking is not to be confused with clear boundary setting within the family context). Mature defences would include appropriate laughter at or rationalisation of our anxieties or foibles. Adolescence is a wonderful time. It is developmentally unique and parents would do well to appreciate the adolescent's defences, however annoying they may be.

Characteristic defences of adolescence are 'acting out' (a typical adolescent defence mechanism specifically explained in Chapter 5), escaping or running away from difficulties, wanting immediate gratification and control, and a sense of supremacy, where they feel or assume that they are invincible. Many defensive actions are triggered as a result of anxiety. Consider for a moment toddlers and how they can feel supreme, where they feel they can do everything, for example, running before they can walk, and how parents encourage them to explore but are there to help them when they fall. Likewise, adolescents believe they are invincible and supreme. While the sense of invincibility can be a positive attitude to have, parents need to protect adolescents from hurting themselves and others. A parent needs to be emotionally present in order to guide the adolescent towards making responsible choices during their displays of perceived omnipotence and supremacy.

At times, both infants and adolescents assume that they are strong enough to command and destroy anything or anyone. In the cycle of life, it is natural and appropriate that the younger generation will one day take over from the older generation. Adolescents sometimes want to expedite the process and take over while they are still in their adolescence. While we believe it certainly is healthy for the adolescent to get a taste of being independent and taking responsibility, it should be remembered that adolescents are not in a position to overthrow their parents (as much as they would like to do so). Adolescents should be given authority and responsibility appropriate to their age.

In adolescence, just as there is a burgeoning of sexuality given the changing body, so there may be an increase in aggressive feelings. Throughout our lives we have to deal with feelings of aggression and how to engage with them; this is true for males and females. A very important consideration, we believe, when parenting an adolescent is to comprehend the inherent 'threat' of adolescence. In infancy there is a free expression of all feelings. For example, an infant can attack and bite their mother's breast or they can love her with an intense passion. In latency, children obey rules and want to please those around them. In adolescence, as in infancy, there is a wish for full expression of emotion and the need for the parents to accept a great deal more around their intensity of emotions. Adolescents are still working through their sexuality and aggression and the consequences of complete free expression are more serious than in infancy.

Aggressive and sexual feelings are normal but need to be channelled in a constructive manner. For example, playing a hard rugby game rather than punching a perceived enemy is a healthy way for the adolescent boy to give expression to his aggressive feelings. Without a physical outlet adolescents who act out their fantasies could cause actual physical harm, whereas in infancy there is little realisable threat to life. It is in this arena where schools can play a significant part in positively directing adolescent energies into sports and other healthy activities.

To help parents understand better management of adolescents in parenting, Winnicott offers some views on adolescence itself. He discusses the shift in power from childhood to adolescence as potentially harmful: 'How shall the adolescent boy or girl deal with the new power to destroy and even kill, a power which did not complicate feelings of hatred at the toddler age? It is like putting new wine in old bottles.' (1961, p 80)

It is therefore vitally important for parents to help their adolescents to channel their hateful or destructive feelings in a constructive manner. Usually the way aggression is dealt with by parents is how adolescents learn to deal with aggression. Fortunately, adolescence is a creative time practically, which allows for opportunities to channel negative energies into various creative areas, for example, plays, poetry, sport, painting, martial arts, yoga and community work. Activities which involve competition, explore idealism and which give expression to the self are useful to healthy development in teenagers.

Adolescents have a more sophisticated thinking ability than when they were in infancy or latency. A maturing intellect can help them deal with their destructive feelings and thoughts in a positive manner. Instead of simply reacting to the emotion, healthy adolescents will be able to make meaningful cognitive links. In addition, since adolescents have developed the thinking capacity for dealing with issues that confront them in everyday living, they are able to reason more effectively and can manage more sophisticated understandings of being rejected by, for example, parents, difficult environments or situations.

In order to consolidate healthy defences, adolescents often need to test their parents. They need to know that their parents can deal with their rage, outbursts and sometimes their incoherent arguments. Parents need to be trusted to hold on to their values and to be firm in the face of bombardment from their adolescent. Being consistent in one's identity and role as a parent helps adolescents develop their own identity more clearly. The parent also teaches adolescents how important it is to collaborate and to relate constructively with people, as this is a vital skill in the adult world. Thoughtful, not perfect, parents can create thoughtful adolescents and in turn thoughtful adults. Adolescents will also learn that they are rarely able to cope with isolation and that we all need community and a sense of belonging and respect for fellow human beings. For adolescents growing up, it means becoming a separate person and moving towards independence. For parents it means allowing the parent-child relationship to move towards a parent-young adult relationship.

Just as a mother cares intensely for the needs of her infant, so too the parent during the initial stages of adolescence needs to take cognisance of the adolescent's preliminary needs for that particular developmental time. For example, adolescents need to be allowed to take more control in their lives. The need for them to feel dominant and strong occasionally should be realised and they need to have a sense that they are being respected when they show that they are needy and fearful, impulsive, fickle with their opinions or confused at times about their identity. Once adolescents have had an experience of a safe place to grapple with uncertain thoughts and feelings, they may be able to manage the disappointment of their sometimes unrealistic expectations of the parent. This helps adolescents to move towards a better management of human relationships.

3. ADOLESCENTS AND THEIR UNIQUE CONNECTION WITH THE SOCIAL WORLD

Winnicott (1961) describes adolescence as a 'doldrums state'. This means they experience a contradiction between needing to respond to an intense, emergency situation, yet simultaneously needing the time to pass slowly. The listlessness of adolescence is caused by the disharmonious experiences of time. It is a very interesting concept, acknowledging that sometimes adolescents need to be separate and isolated from the world – in their room alone, to have the door closed and to be in their own space. For this, adolescents need parents to be respectful of the privacy of this isolation. Although the sense of futility can within reason be a developmentally useful space for adolescents, too much 'doldrumming' is problematic. For example, adolescents who isolate themselves excessively within a cyberspace persona remove themselves from being able to deal with reality.

Winnicott (1961) argues that adolescents are characterised by their immaturity. It is very important for adolescents to be at the level of development that is appropriate for their age and to understand that they are not emotionally mature. For example, it is unhealthy for a young adolescent who is still to get her menstrual cycle, let alone have her first kiss, to be exposed to intimate adult sexual conversation. It would be appropriate for the young adolescent to feel uncomfortable, blush and even feel anxious because she is not a 19 year old who would have developed a more mature understanding of how to cope with the situation. Parents should not expect their young adolescent to be at an older level of development – simply because they are not at that point of development. As adults we need to walk alongside the developmental process and try to encourage healthy, age-appropriate development.

Parents can help their adolescents develop healthily by showing appropriate levels of trust. Trust is critical to any meaningful relationship. Private journals and text messages should, where practical, be respected by parents unless the adolescent has breached trust. In normal, healthy parent-adolescent relationships it is inappropriate and destructive for parents to read journals and private communications undertaken by their adolescents. Doing so can cause significant breaches of trust and interfere with the self-confidence of the adolescent.

It is very normal for adolescents to have fantasies of personal triumph, such as taking over the older generation. Winnicott believed this extreme selfishness and grandiosity was unique to adolescent development. He believed the desire to be victorious, if channelled correctly, was an important attitude to have in order to move towards being a confident, able adult.

Adolescents experience time differently from children and adults, in that they have *intense* physical and emotional surges that make them perceive the moment they are in as *urgent*. This can be likened to Winnicott's 'doldrums state'. A child or adult will have similar experiences, but not necessarily as intensely, owing to their different developmental needs. Adolescents could be described as partly child, partly adult developmentally as a result of how they experience time. The childlike part of the adolescent experiences time as being interminable and the adultlike part experiences needing things to be done quickly, since they perceive time as moving fast.

Adolescents resist the idea that maturing takes a long time because they demand immediate cures and they tend to live in the moment. Roberts (1995) emphasises the importance adolescents attach to experiencing 'immediate' connections and how frustrating maturing is for them. Adolescent development cannot be rushed; it is a matter of development over time. As Winnicott put it: 'Adolescence itself can be a stormy time. Defiance mixed with dependence, even at times extreme dependence, makes the picture of adolescence seem mad and muddled . . . Continuing my sketch of adolescence, dogmatically stated for brevity's sake, there is only one way of treating adolescence, and this is the passage of time and the passing on of the adolescent into the adult state.' (Winnicott, 1963c, pp 242–4)

Parents need to know that adolescents tend to go off track in their development given that they think they know everything and may therefore need a nudge to get back on track. Helping adolescents through the maturational stage and supporting their minor inconsistencies goes some way towards helping them weather the process of growing up. However, when obstacles in life become significantly hard for adolescents to overcome, then outside professional help may be needed.

Winnicott reminds us of the joy of parenting adolescents: 'It is all a problem of *how to be adolescent during adolescence*. This is an extremely brave thing for anybody to be, and some of these people are trying to achieve it. It does not mean that we grown-ups have to be saying: "Look at these dear little adolescents having their adolescence; we must put up with everything and let our windows get broken". That is not the point. The point is that we are challenged, and we meet the challenge as part of the function of adult living. But we meet the challenge rather than set out to cure what is essentially healthy.' (Winnicott, 1961, p 87)

JANUARY

CHANGE AND
NEW BEGINNINGS

The uncertainties for some young adolescents become overwhelming and dominate their sense of stability. In this chapter we look at change and new beginnings and how parents can assist their adolescents at these difficult but significant times.

IT IS A TYPICAL Johannesburg January. The newness of the year is redolent with life and possibility. The holidays, which seemed interminable a few weeks ago, are over and anticipation hangs palpably in the air. New classes, new teachers, new beginnings and, in the case of those entering high school, new 'everythings' are typical for this time of enormous change in the life of an adolescent. Anticipation and anxiety exist in an uneasy alliance. Will the joys of midsummer survive the first day of school? Will the class be all right and will the right friends be there . . . and the teacher? So the anxiety mounts.

Many parents about to embark on the high school experience have agonised over the choice of school for their children. In some cases there is an uninformed hype around the various schools and dinner parties are the peculiar source of much misinformation around how to choose schools. The real stories, of course, remain deeply embedded within each school's hidden history and they are rarely unearthed. Nevertheless, the anxiety around a new start can be compounded for a young adolescent if their parents' anxiety includes the parents' own insecurities about how they will measure up as parents. The three case studies in this chapter look at three different 'beginnings' and how parental involvement can either hamper or enhance the inherent learning experience. The third case looks at the problem of integration into a team and how, as parents, we do not always know what is happening.

CASE STUDY 1: TRANSITION TO HIGH SCHOOL

Georgina was a high-flyer in junior school. She was constantly filled with excitement and happiness at what life had to offer. Academically she was amongst the top achievers in her lively, accomplished group of friends. Besides whizzing through Mathematics and English tests with ease, she was a deft swimmer and an excellent tennis player, besides being recognised for her musical ability. She was focused, popular and her ability and accomplishments were acknowledged by the teachers. While not arrogant, Georgina enjoyed the high-profile status and recognition her talents had brought her. Her parents, quite legitimately, were proud of their daughter's success.

And then along came high school.

Georgina is terrified of the transition to high school. When she goes to bed at night she lies silently wondering if she can sustain her success in the more challenging arena ahead of her. It is a very loud but unspoken fear for parent and child. The more they quietly fret, the bigger the monster grows.

When Georgina arrives at high school on the first day, already anxious, she is overwhelmed by the large number of students and the size of the school. It seems like a labyrinth of corridors and a sense of inadequacy overwhelms her. No one knows her name – she is just another face; she feels insignificant, lost and alone. In primary school her teachers had gone from classroom to classroom; now she will have to find her way around the school according to a timetable. Georgina has to carry her books and her bags are heavy; she has to know what to do each time a bell rings. No longer are the teachers kind and warm. They seem stern, foreign and powerful. Tears are ready to rise up at any moment; it takes energy to keep them in check. There is so much to remember and there are instructions all the time, from not just one kind class teacher, as in junior school, but also from sports teachers, music mistresses and subject teachers. In junior school the class teacher had known everything and had written it up in beautiful block print on the board for her to copy down in her own beautiful block print. Now in high school she doesn't know who to turn to and doesn't have a friend in whom to confide. Her loneliness is new and dark and frightening.

Georgina expresses her anxiety to her mother, who tries valiantly to understand her daughter's experiences and listens carefully, but feels desperate. Fear is a new emotion for Georgina to manage. She is keen to join the school choir, but has to audition. She is keen to try for the tennis team, but has to attend trials. Her skills, once accepted as fact by primary school teachers, are now being tested and even questioned. With her mother's encouragement, she remembers to attend auditions and trials. While fearful of having to pit herself against competition, she works through the new high school processes. Georgina is fortunate to have her mother walking beside her at home, where the support and encouragement she needs are always present.

Although Georgina is successful in the various auditions, she continues to feel lonely and overwhelmed. Five months into the school year, Georgina's mother, surprised and perturbed that her daughter has still not settled into her usual happy state, approaches the school for advice. It is explained to her that not only is her daughter having to cope with a new environment, but she is also having to negotiate new feelings and changes within her identity and her body.

With the combined support of the school and Georgina's parents, additional plans for integration are introduced for her. At the suggestion of the school, Georgina changes classes, not because she cannot get along with those in the group, but rather for the purposes of a metaphorical change for which she is now responsible. In addition, Georgina is encouraged to make friends with those who have similar interests to her. As she slowly makes new friends, Georgina realises that her previous abilities and attributes will always be present to hold her in good stead. It is a matter of having faith in herself and trusting her innate ability.

By the end of the second term of high school, Georgina is flourishing and well on her way to establishing herself as a young woman able to cope with the new demands of high school. Indeed, she will be able to translate the experience positively into any future endeavour in her life because she sees, first hand, the benefits of persevering. Instead of giving up, changing schools, hiding her talents, becoming rebellious and muddled, Georgina has learnt that through negotiation and grappling with the situation and seeking the help of others, she can overcome obstacles. The experience has set Georgina up for future success. She can look back with some degree of satisfaction, knowing that she can manage change and she has gained a valuable life skill that she would not have done had she given up too soon.

Georgina's parents acknowledged their own fear and while they supported their daughter, they also supported the school's attempts to help integrate Georgina successfully into the demands of high school. Georgina made the transition from the little pond to the big pond realising that her abilities would always be present, although she needed to learn to draw on them differently.

CASE STUDY 2: NEW BEGINNINGS FOR A GRADE 10

Alina, an intelligent third-year high school girl, returns to school in January and is unhappy with the class into which she has been placed. Immediately, upon seeing the members of her class, Alina approaches her teacher and demands to be put into a different class group. The teacher, busy with new-year administration, which is significantly onerous at the start of an academic year, tells her that she will look into it in due course to see if a change that suits her subject choice can be made. The teacher cannot address the issue immediately but does not dismiss Alina's complaint entirely. She encourages Alina to try to see the situation through to the end of the day. Instead of hearing the teacher and absorbing her advice, Alina phones her parents on her mobile phone in high anxiety and informs them, through racking sobs, that she has been thrown into a class of miscreants and deviants who are sure to lead her astray.

As she speaks she becomes increasingly hysterical, and before the morning's welcome assembly can begin, Alina is whisked to the safety of her home by a compliant mother who immediately assumes the school is at fault. At home Alina's mother escalates the problem by informing her husband that the 'terrible school' has betrayed their daughter.

The father, burly and powerful, incensed by the pain his daughter displays, immediately sets to putting the situation right for his daughter. He shoots off a lengthy rude email to the school principal demanding that his daughter be placed in a class of her choice. He lambastes the school for their lack of care and concern and threatens to withdraw Alina from the school.

Alina had been placed in the specific class group on account of the subjects she had chosen. A good school, or even a 'good enough' school, would not deliberately place an achieving, compliant student into a class against the student's wishes. Students are placed into class groups around ability, subject choice and class size. Very rarely would a student be placed in a class for reasons other than logistics or for the individual student's progress and development. Schools want the students in their care to thrive and flourish. A good school will place a student in a class where the school feels the individual will gain the maximum benefit from the learning process. It is unlikely that parents will be fully aware of all the ramifications that go into placing a student in a specific class. From time to time a school may well separate a particular student from a certain peer group in an attempt to engender new developments and new understandings. Good schools will never deliberately try to lessen a student's progress. Good schools want and need their students to thrive and they avoid unnecessary conflict.

Alina changed her subjects so that she could move to a class with her friends. By allowing Alina to have her way and change her subjects for so whimsical a reason, her parents compromised the relationship with the school by reacting rudely and by assuming the school's intentions were misguided. Alina's manipulation was rewarded by her parents, who perceived her as having been badly treated.

Instead of acting immediately to Alina's unhappiness and responding, ironically, much in the way an adolescent would in a situation of change, Alina's parents would have done well to have stepped back from the situation. Rather than reacting to the adolescent tantrum by having their own tantrum, they could have taught Alina to think through the process and step aside from it for a while. They did not have to deny her unhappiness, but they could have provided her with skills to approach the school herself and to negotiate a solution that was to her benefit.

Adolescents often respond with immediacy to a given situation. Their insistency raises issues to a level of urgency and anxiety. As adults, we need to encourage them to think through their concerns calmly and to react in a considered manner. Alina needed to think through the issue of changing subjects to suit her friends far more carefully. Making an issue out of something so trivial could change the course of her life.

An opportunity to learn important skills for life was lost because of rash actions on the part of the parents. Interestingly, Alina continued to stage-manage her parents far more significantly during the course of the year, particularly around her social life, and by the end of the year a once compliant, achieving student was leading a social life far removed from what her parents expected of her.

CASE STUDY 3: NEW BEGINNINGS IN A TEAM – INITIATION OR INTEGRATION?

Matthew is an athletic, handsome, well-built 15 year old at a top school. He is an exceptional sportsman. In spite of his age but on account of his extraordinary ability, Matthew is selected to play first-team cricket. An exciting new beginning – or so he thinks. There is an overt and a covert integration process into the team. The overt integration requires Matthew to be the 'team skivvy'. The covert activity is more sinister and requires Matthew to be smacked with the team's symbolic cricket bat on his buttocks or thighs by at least one of the established team members.

Ostensibly this is a rite of passage that 'makes him a man'. His father, had he spoken to him, would in all likelihood have been right behind the process. Matthew, nervous but determined to show the older boys he is 'a man', bends over to receive the 'welcome' blow. The blow is wielded with an unexpected and nasty ferocity and he winces as the bat side swipes his thigh with a resounding 'thwack'. Terrified he is going to cry, he remains bent for a few extra seconds in order to compose himself. He manages to drag a grin onto his face and deny his tormentors the joy of his pain, but he cannot walk back to his place easily and his hobble is met with derisive laughter and comments about his arrogance.

For a few days Matthew tells no one about the event. A few days later, at another sporting event, Matthew discloses his pain to another coach outside of his school. The coach sees the spidering bruise creeping out from below the hem of his shorts and expresses indignation at the force of a blow which could cause not only such a long bruise but also such a deep angry purple. In spite of the coach's protestations, Matthew begs the coach not to tell his mother because he is sure she will go to the school authorities and cause him further embarrassment and more humiliation, and possibly more physical pain. The coach reluctantly agrees not to intervene.

This type of activity is unacceptable and in this particular instance it is interesting to note that it served to curtail Matthew's participation in school sport.

Integration, at the time of new beginnings, is a complex concept. Integration activities into a school or a team should be short-lived, kind and inclusive. The physical and psychological integrity of an individual should not be compromised by the actions of another, and in the case of Matthew it may be argued that his human rights were breached. There is no shortage of positive exercises that can assist students getting to know one another. Anything that deviates from the positive aims of integration should see parents stepping in to guide their adolescents. If integration processes exist within a school they should be nurturing and safe for the students and the actions benign. The events should build trust and respect and should never be left to older students to administer unless they are closely supervised by adults.

DEVELOPMENTAL CONSIDERATIONS AND SUGGESTIONS

As a parent, you will know how your adolescent normally responds to change and whether change leads to anxiety. Whether the change is from primary school to high school or from the penultimate to the final year at school, or simply from one class to another, change has an impact. Moving from the top of primary school to the bottom of senior school, as in the case of Georgina, can leave adolescents feeling a little downsized. Parents in this situation need to be alert to their adolescent's feelings until the adolescent feels strong enough to be more independent in the situation.

Let's consider Alina's case. Acting out her anxiety by attacking the school, Alina's parents do not help her to learn to take responsibility for her fears and her own development. Protecting your adolescents without rescuing them shows that you care and are aware of their perceived pain. Reflecting the emotions that are being expressed by the adolescents back to them allows parents to resonate with the adolescent without controlling the experience.

As a parent, your behaviour and emotional response to your adolescent's cry for help requires careful thought. A useful question to ask when responding to your adolescent's angst is: *Is this a parent, adolescent or school issue?*

For example, is it a parent issue where the parent is struggling with the realisation that the adolescent is no longer a child who was easy to protect; does the parent feel threatened by the prospect of not being able to protect the adolescent and so feels disempowered? Or is the problem in fact an adolescent issue, where the parent knows or senses that there are underlying emotional difficulties with which the adolescent is grappling? Does the adolescent complain too often or have low self-esteem that needs to be addressed? Or third, is it a school issue where the institution may have misunderstood or failed to support the adolescent and the parent may need to intervene or seek support from the school?

To illustrate, Georgina's parents were prepared to acknowledge their own anxiety in relation to Georgina's transition to high school and were prepared to seek help for Georgina to manage her own concerns that the change of environment caused. Conversely, Alina's parents needed to be more aware that their own anxieties spilt over into their daughter's exaggerated disappointment and they exacerbated the situation and prevented an opportunity for development to take place. In Matthew's case the school failed him and ought to have been alerted to the damage it was inadvertently causing through the actions of other students. Matthew's parents, if they had noticed any significant behavioural changes, should have sought advice. If they were alert, they could have investigated why their son's attitude to sport had changed.

From a developmental point of view and in the context of change, Georgina needed to complete the change cycle more effectively before negotiating the challenge of high school. Typically in change, there is the paradox of gain and loss. Georgina needed consciously to mourn the loss of junior school and all it represented to her, while understanding and embracing the possibilities that existed within high school. Schools and parents would do well to prepare young people for these unavoidable and obvious changes that take place. (Chapter 7 deals more thoroughly with the subject of loss.) As adults we cannot ignore the depth of loss felt by adolescents when they move schools, change teachers or when their friends leave them. There are many instances of boys who were top in sports teams in their junior schools and whose size lets them down at the start of high school. This change of hierarchy can be keenly felt. Some parents, particularly fathers, can become critical of their sons who do not make top teams as they enter high school and this can have devastating consequences for the relationship Boys who have ability but lack strength because of their physique can be encouraged to train in order to compensate for their physical shortcomings, but this must not be done at the expense of their other attributes or against their will. Not everyone can be the best and not everyone can be in the top teams. All these events that trigger a sense of loss can cause insecurity in the young adolescent's sense of self. (Physical body issues will be more fully covered in Chapter 9.)

In certain situations anxiety is appropriate. Occasionally parents feel the need to mitigate anxiety to the point where they prevent the potential development inherent in the anxiety. If your adolescent is generally very anxious, notice which responses usually help the adolescent feel in control and supported and employ these if possible.

For example, perhaps Alina's parents know from past experience that she exaggerates situations and they need to listen to her fears but trust that she is not being neglected by the school. Unless the school has regularly let them down, parents should trust their choice of school. Alternatively, in Alina's case, the father may know that he struggles with anxiety, particularly when others around him are anxious, and that he needs to monitor how he responds to the anxieties of others.

As a parent, try to look for defences in yourself and in your adolescent. Encourage healthy responses to unwanted emotions such as nervousness or fear. For example, it is healthy to acknowledge and name the defences that we develop in ourselves in order for the behaviour to be recognised and dealt with, rather than being accepted as an appropriate default emotion to which the adolescent can cling regardless of the efficacy of the defence. Thinking through experiences and problems is a useful lifelong skill for an adolescent to acquire.

Alina's parents missed an opportunity to help Alina to evaluate her thinking. Alina did not consider other possibilities, nor did her parents guide her to do so. No attempt was made to explore the reasons behind her placement in the class. Alina immediately defaulted to overreacting and assuming that she had been dealt with unfairly. A calm analysis of the circumstances would have gone a long way in helping Alina deal with her anxieties and to cope better with the next anxious situation.

Acknowledge the anxieties your adolescents may feel. Try to

encourage them to name these fears. By naming their fear they gain a measure of control over the emotion. Remember, developmentally, the importance of belonging is crucial to an adolescent and if they fear that this will be compromised in any way, they may react as Alina did.

Explaining to your adolescents that they need to learn to grapple with frightening or painful emotions is valuable because it will help them to develop better insight into their feelings. With greater insight comes greater confidence in dealing with and acknowledging their emotions. Your adolescents may react negatively to your suggestions at first. Although they may appear to fob off your advice, your ideas will invariably germinate in moments of quietness and reflection. An adolescent can integrate different ideas into their thinking but they will rarely be able to admit to embracing a parent's advice.

With the tangible loss of a previous school context or a change of grade comes an opportunity for emotional development in trusting new spaces and oneself in those spaces. Not only parents but also peers are important during adolescence since it is a time when adolescents need to be separating from their parents. Equally, teachers and significant adults need to be aware of their role when an adolescent confides in them. In Matthew's case he was let down.

In addition there should not be secrets in the school or the parent community if it entails excluding someone, unless of course it is to give joy to someone. Parents and teachers can ask themselves why the situation needs to be a secret and if it is not to offer kindness to the person, then the secret should not be perpetuated. The secret around Matthew's integration was the first sign that something was amiss.

Matthew would have been counting on the process to bring him closer to a sense of belonging within the team. If the process had helped Matthew respect the need for authority in life while simultaneously showing him that, as an individual, he was a valuable part of the team, the process would have been valuable. But Matthew had not been integrated effectively; rather he had been let down significantly. By not confronting the school, the coach in whom Matthew confided unintentionally colluded with the unacceptable behaviour of the other team members. The coach should have considered whether it was ethically in the best interests of Matthew not to address the humiliation he had felt. The school should have been alerted to the issue without compromising Matthew's integrity. Adolescents need to be supported by adults through the growing up process.

Change, in various forms, is an inevitable part of life. Adolescents may feel the effects of change keenly and it is our responsibility as adults to help them negotiate, rather than avoid, the change so that it can lead to positive development.

SUMMING UP

- Change brings growth and a chance for development.

- Embrace change by talking about the inherent paradox of change – the gains and losses that exist in all change.

- Discuss losses that have occurred in your family. Consider the opportunities as well as the pain that have resulted from these losses.

- Stand behind processes within schools that are there to support your adolescent and reject all instances where adolescents are undermined.

- Ask: Is this a parental issue, an adolescent issue or a school issue? Then respond accordingly.

FEBRUARY

2

LOVE AND HATE

Adolescents feel emotions of love and hate intensely. In this chapter we consider the very real and deep feelings adolescents have when they are in love and the destructive, hateful emotions that they can experience and that are often denied existence.

FEBRUARY IS HOT AND sultry and on some days the heat can be oppressive. In the Western world it is the month typically associated with love, centring around Valentine's Day. Those adolescents that are in love celebrate February with the abundant joy that attends the beauty inherent in first or young love.

Yet, paradoxically, Valentine's Day holds the potential for being one of the cruellest days of the year on some adolescents' calendars. Not, of course, that an adolescent would easily confess to any significant anxiety around the fourteenth of February. Consumerist society has ensured that no one forgets that Valentine's Day exists. On Valentine's Day, our lookist, consumerist society martyrs hundreds of fragile psyches at the altar of conformity and consumer hype. Perhaps the blatant violation against St Valentino, the Christian martyr cruelly executed centuries ago, is not so far removed from the violations against less robust adolescents today.

While there is excitement and joy for some, there is also a sadness, often hidden from view, that pervades the hot February air. On Valentine's Day many adolescents fear being labelled, judged inadequate, publicly humiliated and have an overwhelming sense of being 'unloved' because the day creates expectations and raises hopes.

Although love and hate are emotions that occur throughout the year, Valentine's Day often highlights the emotions felt by adolescents.

CASE STUDY 4: BURGEONING LOVE AND SEXUALITY

The sun is shining. Jessica skips happily along. Jeremy is gorgeous. She cannot believe he is hers. Even the hymns she sings in chapel remind her of her wonderful boyfriend. She has never felt like this before; no boy has moved her to feel what she feels. Physically she feels more alive than ever. Her skin glows and her life seems as close to perfect as she dare dream.

Her peers are envious of Jessica as she floats to lessons on the tip of Cupid's wings. 'If music be the food of love, play on'; she thinks the teacher has chosen Orsino's words just for her. Immediately *Twelfth Night* is her favourite play. The Elizabethan music in the distant background of her mind conflates with her thoughts.

When Jessica arrives home she has a letter from Jeremy. A real-life love letter! The hand-delivered letter is poetically penned and further proof for her that Jeremy is perfect. Homework is accomplished in less than no time because she is motivated to write a reply to Jeremy. She also writes an English essay with the title 'If music be the food of love, play on'.

Walking past her mother's room, Jessica feels compelled to eavesdrop on a phone conversation her mother is having with Jeremy's mother. It seems as if the latter is concerned that Jeremy is 'in love'. The parents battle through the territory of teenage love with each other and Jessica smiles. She wants to butt in and yell triumphantly, 'Of course it is real!' But she smiles and leaves the mothers to commiserate with each other across the telephone lines.

A few days later her joy is compounded by success. Her English teacher is delighted with the essay she had written and Jessica is equally pleased with the comment made and the symbol given by the teacher at the end of the essay. Love certainly isn't compromising her academic triumphs!

After dating Jeremy for an entire term, Jessica bubbles with excitement when her mother agrees to let her spend a long weekend with Jeremy and his parents at a holiday resort. Before setting off, Jessica's mother gives her the proverbial mother-daughter lecture but Jessica cannot take it in as she imagines four entire heavenly days with her boyfriend. Motherly words of wisdom are as insubstantial as air when they are spoken at the wrong time.

Jessica has a wonderful time with Jeremy and his parents, save for one incident which sends her into deep confusion. The perfect feeling is a little tainted and Jessica is unsure what to do with her feelings. She wants to talk to her mother but can't. She wants to talk to her friends but doesn't want them to judge her. There is no doubt that she still adores Jeremy but things are different and her mother senses a change in her but is too afraid to broach the subject.

A few days after the weekend away, still confused, Jessica finds her English teacher during a free lesson and asks her to read a poem she has written. The poem reveals her confusion about having gone too far with Jeremy. After the teacher has read the poem, Jessica confides in her that they haven't had sex but they have certainly explored each other's bodies intimately.

'No one warned me that it would be so nice,' she confesses. 'I am so scared I won't be able to stop the next time we are alone. Why didn't someone warn me that the feeling would be so powerful? I feel completely out of control and I don't want to have sex while I am at school. When Jeremy said sorry he had gone so far, I wanted to say but why say sorry, it was so fabulous. But then I realised it must be wrong.'

'It's not wrong, so much as the wrong time,' suggests the teacher; and so begins a rare and important conversation.

Often adolescents are taught to fear their sexuality and their intense feelings of love and the subject is rarely broached meaningfully. The intensity of their feelings is often relegated to clichés rather than understood.

CASE STUDY 5: RECEIVING A HATEFUL MESSAGE

In some schools there is a tradition in the name of fund-raising that encourages adolescents to send plastic roses to each other on Valentine's Day. Not receiving a rose on one's first significant Valentine's Day can be felt as a huge disappointment, to which there will be varying degrees of reaction and soul-searching. Usually the pain of perceived rejection is short-lived, perhaps even laughed about in years to come, but when roses are sent with cruel messages, the pain can be unbearable.

Valentine's Day comes round and it has been an acutely bad morning at home for Jemma. She is not particularly concerned about the day ahead. Love, or any shallow references to it, is hardly in the forefront of her mind as her parents have been ranting and screaming at each other; there is no doubt that they are getting ready for a divorce. Jemma is dropped off at school and thinks that she will receive some respite from the chaos at home.

A break from the monotony of lessons arrives and the students are summonsed by senior students to go to the school hall. If they have been sent a rose from one of the neighbouring schools their names will be called out publicly and amongst much festivity and shrieking they have to walk to the stage to fetch the so-called symbol of love. The popular students receive rose after rose; the less popular get none. Jemma is surprised to hear her name called and she shyly walks towards the outstretched hand wielding the plastic Valentine's rose. Momentarily her heart skips a beat and she blushes with delight that someone has thought of her. However, her brief flutter of happiness is short-lived. The anonymous message attached to the green plastic stem screams its hatred at her: 'Even if you were the last loser on earth I wouldn't pick you.'

It is not difficult for anyone to understand that a young adolescent tussling with issues around identity and relationships is going to struggle to see this type of cruel and silly message for what it really is. In this case the consequences were reasonably severe. Jemma tried to run away from home and school and felt disproportionate embarrassment.

CASE STUDY 6: BOYS IN LOVE

Charles is 17. He is comfortable with himself and happy with life in general. One of his joys is his girlfriend, Ruth. He has been going out with Ruth for a whole year. He invited her out on Valentine's Day the year before and he enjoyed the steadiness of one girlfriend. Together they share secrets and laughter, fears and hopes, and occasionally they do homework together and share notes. When she isn't busy she watches his rugby matches and he watches her netball games. All in all it is a happy, healthy relationship.

The parents of Charles and Ruth support the relationship, although they maintain fairly strict rules and boundaries. Each of the adolescents feels comfortable in the home of the other.

To celebrate the milestone of going out for a whole year, Charles decides to spoil Ruth. He asks his mother to prepare a special dinner for the two of them to be served in the garden under the stars. Delighted to be involved in his expression of care and love for his girlfriend, Charles's mother plans a menu for the two young lovers. A table is beautifully decorated and set out on the lawn in the garden. Candlelight and elegant cutlery add to the romantic effect. In addition to the dinner, Charles buys flowers for Ruth and organises for his little sister to stand on a stool at the front door and shower Ruth with fragrant petals when she enters.

Ruth is completely taken by the romantic element to her spoiling and admits to being surprised by the thoughtfulness that has gone into the evening.

DEVELOPMENTAL CONSIDERATIONS AND SUGGESTIONS

The powerful emotions experienced by adolescents are significant. They can love and hate intensely. The way love and hate are experienced and expressed by adolescents can be influenced by the parents' way of living and their way of dealing with love and hate.

Loving emotions are easier to manage than hateful feelings. There is much that can be positively adapted from the strong, loving emotions that adolescents can feel. If harnessed effectively, their love for others can be channelled into effective work in the broader community. Adolescent boys, contrary to the stereotype, can be sensitive and caring and it is worth helping them acknowledge and develop these feelings of connectedness. By allowing boys to display affection, as in the case of Charles in Case Study 6, they develop the ability to build strong relationships and so become caring, sensitive adults. Boys, including big, brave tough ones, should be allowed to cry or be sentimental. Boys can and do feel deeply and can be badly hurt by girls as much as girls can be hurt by the actions of boys when they are in a relationship. Importantly, adults have to avoid trivialising adolescent relationships.

Often adolescents' loving emotions are transferred into loving relationships, which need to be managed rather than feared by parents. In the case of Jessica in Case Study 4 of this chapter, both her parents and Jeremy's parents could acknowledge the poignancy and the power around a first meaningful relationship. Where possible, parents should try to celebrate the maturing sexuality of their children without condoning promiscuity. In order to understand your adolescents, reflect on your own early romantic interludes.

Besides recollections of early love, parents and adolescents need to recognise that adolescents are physically ready to reproduce but are not emotionally ready. If parents and adolescents, together, can acknowledge the hard task this conflict presents them, they will be in a better position to deal with the topic. Some teenage pregnancies could be avoided if parents acknowledged that the adolescent's sexuality is very strong at this time and physically it is normal for their bodies and emotions to be fully charged. Recognising that they are not yet in a position to be parents themselves means that adolescents have to take responsibility for how they express themselves physically and emotionally. Parents may also remind their adolescents of their values and spiritual beliefs and how their behaviour confirms their beliefs. It is also a time to discuss contraception and the consequences of pregnancy, HIV/AIDS and other sexually transmitted infections. Ignoring the powerful sexual feelings experienced by most adolescents is to be unaware and naive.

Monitoring peer pressure is also helpful and discussions around sex need to be had. Invariably, adolescents do not want to have sex education from their parents but rather they want to have more generalised discussions. Adolescents do not like to think of their parents having sex. They tend to see their parents as asexual. However this does not let parents off the hook and parents cannot bury their heads in the sand – it is a fact that many adolescents are having sex. Be pragmatic but instil values in your adolescent.

Fathers are very important in the process of a daughter developing her sexual identity. It is no coincidence that the concept 'daughters look for their fathers in their lovers' is widely recognised. Parents need to make sure that the adolescent girl does not override the mother or get in the middle of the parent couple. The same applies for an adolescent boy. Initially, such an experience can excite an adolescent girl; however, significant anxiety can arise since the adolescent girl realises that her place is not to be the 'wife'. It threatens her sense of security. Adolescent girls in their early teens sometimes explain how their fathers stop hugging and kissing them. It is normal for a father to think his daughter is attractive. Some fathers describe feeling anxious about their feelings so they withdraw, which is not helpful to the adolescent girl.

Parents must remain parents. Mothers occasionally feel that they are in competition with their daughters, who invariably surpass the mother with their youth and looks, and again it is about appreciating their development rather than starting to dress in adolescent clothes and engage in competitive behaviour. To do so is to forego being the parent and to become a sexualised, inappropriate mother. The same can be said of fathers who try to compete physically with the growing strength of adolescent sons.

Parents need to think about what is valuable about their marital relationship and what does not work. As adolescents get older, parents are able to be more honest about what does not work and that relationships do not have to be perfect, but that sometimes it is about *how* to be in the relationship that results in a positive loving experience. As the adolescent develops and separates into independence, so he or she will take what is perceived as valuable and then integrate their own unique beliefs about a loving relationship.

As parents, just as we need to understand the intensity of love, we need to understand the power of and the place for hateful emotions. When younger children articulate intense dislike or hate, they are often socialised into denying these hateful emotions. Where do those emotions go? We cannot ignore the power that lies in unmanaged, extreme emotions.

We all have the capacity to love and hate. When a person is able to moderate the hateful, destructive feelings with love they can be said to be mature. In psychotherapy, for example, hate is not denied but rather understood.

Life is a long journey of being able to integrate the loving and hateful emotions within ourselves. In infancy, loving and hateful feelings are expressed by the infant and tolerated by the mother. For example, the infant may go red in the face and feel like harming its parents when it feels angry and frustrated. In adolescence, the powerful emotions of love and hate are similar. The adolescent's capacity to cause physical damage and to be destructively violent or verbally vindictive has much greater consequences than the anger of an infant.

We are often not allowed to acknowledge the hateful part of ourselves and so we sometimes resort to 'acting out' (discussed more fully in Chapter 5) which is explained in Case Study 5, for example. By sending a cruel, hateful message to Jemma, rather than acknowledging his desire for power and his need for the expression of personal difficult emotions, the sender of the message hurts Jemma significantly and dangerously. The acting out of the emotions fails to resolve the obvious anger the adolescent feels and he viciously transfers his hatred onto another. This is typical when one cannot cope with one's own inadequacy and in psychology this is termed 'projection'. The boy's message to Jemma reflected his own damaged, unattractive sense of self.

In adolescence, when personality structures are fluid, adolescents project what they hate onto other people because the feeling is too unbearable for them to own. When the boy finds his thoughts about his own unattractiveness intolerable, he temporarily gets rid of them by sending the message to Jemma. He then feels better within himself because he has made somebody else feel hateful.

Adolescents often feel compelled to keep their thoughts separate. For example, when they have good news, the whole world is their best friend. They do not believe or understand that there can be any continuity between having this *best* feeling on their *worst* day, so they disconnect any possibility that love and hate can co-exist within themselves.

As a parent you may wish to consider times when you project your own dissatisfactions, or other feelings, onto others, including those close to you or even onto teachers and schools. By understanding our own human foibles we can empathise more competently with adolescents. Because of the fluid nature of the adolescent personality structure, we need to empathise with them since they are working towards integrating these conflicting and often paradoxical emotions. During this process, adolescents can behave self-centredly or even narcissistically. Parents can help their adolescents by acknowledging that these passionate and disparate emotions exist within the adolescent. Once again, parents are encouraged to shield their adolescents from these stormy times by understanding, not necessarily accepting, their behaviour. If adolescents feel safe to express their emotions to their parents, they will display and express these hateful emotions in an appropriate space and be able to move beyond them. This may well be a very trying and potentially hurtful period for parents to manage. Often parents avoid confrontations where these emotions are likely to be displayed because they can degenerate into catastrophic, exhausting and angry experiences. While violence can never be condoned, acknowledgement of angry clashes can be healthy and useful if reflected upon quietly after the tension of the conflict has passed.

Encourage adolescents to let off steam either verbally or in healthy recreational activities. When there are no healthy alternatives to counterbalance these extreme – but often real – emotions, adolescents might resort to acting out their feelings. For example, they may engage in risk-taking behaviour, which can manifest itself in abusing substances, drinking alcohol excessively or engaging in physical fights or careless sexual activity. Conversely, it must also be understood that the adolescent who withdraws from dealing with the conflicting, powerful emotions is also susceptible to destructive activities, such as substance abuse, cutting and other disordered behaviour. They can be said to be taking their destructive feelings out on themselves rather than projecting them onto others. It is therefore important for adolescents to understand and have the space to deal appropriately with negative feelings.

Parents need to remain adult when adolescent personalities are so fluid and are encouraged to remember that adolescents need a strong parent in order to practise their expression and understanding of unwanted emotions. Adolescents will most likely defend against the emotion of hate, given the difficulties associated with expressing negative feelings. It is therefore important to discuss and raise the concept of normal hateful emotions and to understand and channel these feelings. There is a fine balance between taking adolescents seriously and not being overwhelmed by them. If relationships between parents are constructive when dealing with difficult emotions, then adolescents will often deal with difficult emotions in a similar manner; concomitantly, if parents deal with hate physically or are emotionally violent, then adolescents may well take the cue to act in a similar manner to their parents.

Adolescents are intensely physical in their development. Parents need to be empathetic towards their feeling physically awkward and sometimes even feeling alien to themselves. This physical state, combined with intense emotional and often sexual feelings, is bound to result in occasional explosive behaviour. For example, adolescents feel immortal and powerful and owing to their immaturity they are capable of impulsively hurting others. This happens largely because adolescents are not yet comfortable with the skill of owning their own conflicting emotions.

Adolescents can feel incredibly embarrassed – excruciatingly so – for their 'stupid' behaviour and they may need their parents to help them 'save face'; in other words, parents need to help their adolescents separate their behaviour from themselves in order to look at the behaviour in a more manageable way. Parents need to prepare for the turbulence caused by these conflicting, paradoxical emotions and be solid during the storm that inevitably ensues. It does not matter what kind of family you are: single, gay, heterosexual or divorced. What matters is how you deal with the feelings that the adolescent displays. The key is to be the solid, consistent adult while your adolescent is in this state of fluidity.

School resources can help adolescents channel powerful emotions constructively by offering outlets for these emotions. For example, with hateful, destructive emotions, energy can be given an outlet in sport or in activities that channel the attention of adolescents and thus help them deal with their emotions.

Some individuals struggle to integrate their loving and hateful selves during adolescence. By way of caution, therefore, if parents believe that they have done all that is possible and their adolescent is still behaving dangerously, then professional intervention may be needed. Parents should not be embarrassed to go and see a psychologist, or someone at the school, if they feel that their adolescent's move towards adulthood is being compromised or complicated in any way.

The example a parent sets around issues of love and hate is significant, since thoughts and experiences of love and hate as a parent will impact on how your adolescent understands and relates to these powerful emotions.

SUMMING UP

- Debate and talk about hate and love in order to manage these emotions.

- In times of high conflict, try to remain the adult, but in quieter, more reflective moments admit your hurt and your own shortcomings.

- While adolescents may enjoy discussing relationships and romantic relationships, they will not necessarily want overt sex education from their parents. Parents must, however, be aware that many adolescents are having sex and that discussion around values, contraception and HIV/AIDS and other sexually transmitted infections should be had.

- Adolescent boys are capable of sensitive and romantic feelings. They should be encouraged to acknowledge them and they should not be mocked for their sentiments.

- If integration of emotions seems fraught and disorders appear, seek professional help.

3

MARCH

DISAPPOINTMENT, MIRRORING AND THE NEED FOR REFLECTION

Disappointment is as normal to living as is breathing, and yet parents often try desperately to shield their children from disappointment. Parents sometimes look for excuses rather than substantive reasons when adolescents do not achieve what they want them to achieve. In this chapter we look at how the parents' disappointment and expectations may reflect their own concerns and consequently inhibit their adolescent's development.

WITH MARCH COME SETTLED, bright blue skies, punctuated by fluffy white clouds. Rain showers are occasional. The school term is equally settled and stable, perhaps getting a little dull for adolescents, who are yearning for a break from the perceived monotony of school. Some parents, too, are feeling the need for relief from school more acutely than others and commiserate with their offspring's longing for the term to end.

CASE STUDY 7: INAPPROPRIATE REFLECTIONS

Skye slides into the principal's office. Her hair is dyed a gaudy red and her dress is hitched up in a desperate attempt to be defiant and trendy. Her black lace-up school shoes have not seen polish for some time and the backs have been trodden down so that they appear to be slip-ons. Adolescent disgruntlement is her mantle. Beneath the veneer, and traces of dark make-up that hasn't been removed properly, her pretty eyes search desperately for a recognition she pretends she doesn't want.

She has been sent to the principal by a stern teacher who is usually well able to maintain discipline. With a charming frankness, Skye informs the principal of the reason she has been sent. An assignment has not been completed in spite of several requests to do so. There is no lack of confidence in her attitude and she oozes adolescent ennui.

She says she had trouble with the group with whom she was working, then attached herself to another group and became muddled along the way. Skye is perceptive enough to recognise the work-avoidance behaviour and is gracious enough at this point not to challenge why the teacher didn't push her harder through the process. Asked if this is the only reason she has been sent to the principal, she sheepishly grins and explains that she has been disruptive by encouraging other students to look at a book she had brought to class. The book is about her hero – a wealthy American fashion icon. She bravely acknowledges that the main reason she needs to be chastised is that she has disrupted other people's learning.

It is agreed that she will apologise to the teacher and that the book will be confiscated. Skye balks at this punishment since it is not her book but her older sister's. In spite of her pleas to have the book returned to her, she is told emphatically that she has to realise the consequences of her actions. Skye reluctantly accepts the punishment and shambles out of the principal's office.

Later that afternoon Skye's mother arrives, without an appointment, at the principal's office. It is a hot, muggy Friday and she has to wait. An hour later she totters into the office on her high stiletto heels and demands the return of the book. Her tight pants defy the signs of imminent aging.

The principal has to assess whether refusing to return the book is being mean and manipulative or whether she has Skye's best interests at heart. She decides it is the latter. The mother is aghast at the principal's reply of 'No. Skye needs to learn a lesson.'

'But it's not her book,' defends the mother.

'Even more then the reason she should have been more careful with someone else's property.'

'You mean to say I will be without the book for the weekend?'

The principal nods.

Quite unexpectedly the mother begins to cry 'How am I going to tell my girls they can't have the book for the weekend.'

The principal's facetious reply, 'Girls, you can't have the book for the weekend,' is met with further angry tears.

The mother is furious when she leaves, objecting that the school has no right to impose its values onto her. She is determined that the school is deliberately out to be difficult. The sound of her stilettos down the corridor taps out her indignation.

It is evident from her outburst that this mother wants to protect her children. For her, the significance in her parenting is to make everything perfect and easy, therefore denying the culpability of the adolescent. She wants to give the adolescents the pot of gold at the end of the rainbow without making them manage the journey. Rainbows occur after storms. Sometimes the gold is the lesson learnt from getting wet and experiencing the rain.

CASE STUDY 8: POOR BEHAVIOUR IS NOT ALWAYS WHAT IT SEEMS

Sitting in the office of the headmaster at an upmarket school, Thabo, gaunt with worry, does not know how to answer the headmaster's angry question, 'Do you know that CCTV cameras do not lie?'

The headmaster asks Thabo if he would like to see the incriminating video clip and Thabo knows this means he is in deep trouble. He feels the opportunities he has been given flying out the window next to the headmaster's desk. Thabo, a Grade 9 student, is on a programme that offers very intelligent underprivileged children an opportunity of excellent education. The deal is simple and he has broken it. Students need to perform well academically and follow the school's code of conduct.

Absolute terror churns in the pit of his stomach as he now considers the consequences of his actions. With sweaty palms and tightened facial muscles, adrenalin pumping in his chest, Thabo sees nothing for it but to confess to the headmaster that he has stolen a cellphone and money from his peers. His mouth is dry, his mind like a gyrating spinning top, as he realises the imminent decision the school will make about his fate. The rancid smell of fear permeates the room. He knows the options are expulsion, suspension or rehabilitation, depending on his emotional state, and his sponsors will be informed of his transgression. The disappointment his sponsors will feel will be difficult to manage, and his parents will probably disown him.

Bursting to be understood and heard, Thabo decides to tell his story; after all, he has already lost face. He lives with his parents and six additional people in a very small two-bedroomed house in Gugulethu. Two years ago he had been offered the scholarship and he is very grateful for the learning experience, but the programme also makes him feel inadequate as a person. Labelled as a financially poor black person, he feels he is always required to behave in a respectful, humble way that makes him uncomfortable. Embarrassed, he explains that his family do not have their own transport, so attending evening functions at school is very difficult.

Thabo explains the added pressure from his family members, who are clinging to his success to give them hope for the future. Living in a home with no quiet area or space to study makes it almost impossible to complete all the homework effectively. At school he feels that his marks are scrutinised to ensure that he is achieving the marks that will keep him in the programme, while at home he is scrutinised to ensure that he will bring new hope to the family while not adopting arrogant habits. Wealthy black students resent him and often carelessly comment on his township manners. His own feelings and needs are irrelevant and ignored.

Thabo goes on to explain how the school misinterprets his parents' lack of response to compulsory school parent functions: 'Please understand that my mom and dad are so embarrassed to be seen here with how they look and how they speak. They have lived in a shack all their lives and have no idea how to eat scones with jam and cream at a parents' get-together.'

One and a half years of feeling disillusioned with not doing things the way he apparently should, and experiencing being 'dressed up' as a privileged boy but going home every evening to very poor conditions, have left Thabo feeling desperate.

'It's like living in two different worlds with no clear identity to hold on to,' he tells the headmaster, at last unleashing his deep and real anxiety. In his pain, the truth tumbles out to the listening ears. 'I'm sure you've heard of the "coconut", well I'm a "top deck". I feel like a whitey at school and a darky at home. I feel so empty inside about who I really am, I became angry and decided to just take from people … just like they do to me. I have a phone. I didn't need the phone; I just took it.'

Listening to and believing Thabo's despair, the headmaster is in a dilemma as he grapples between the need to teach the consequences of actions and yet to also understand the troubling and significant reasons that were at the root of Thabo's delinquent behaviour. It is obvious that Thabo feels lost and disrespected for who he really is. From the conversation it has become clear that the young adolescent despises himself and feels that there is little point to living, since he feels he can't and doesn't belong in either world.

The headmaster decides to provide Thabo with a committed mentor, whom Thabo has to see on a weekly basis. He gives Thabo a school punishment that requires physical hard work and makes him face the peers from whom he has stolen and ask them for a second chance to establish trust. He gives Thabo another chance to prove himself. Besides the mentoring, Thabo also has to commit to seeing the school psychologist regularly.

Once he has made the decision, the headmaster leans back in his chair and contemplates the irate phone calls he will no doubt receive from parents, telling him he should be made of sterner stuff, but he is the one who has to live with his decision and this will be Thabo's last and only reprieve.

CASE STUDY 9 AND 10: TO WHOM DOES THE DISAPPOINTMENT BELONG?

Susan Jones's mother sees the principal in the car park and snarls, 'I hate looking at you and what you represent.' Trying to diffuse the bitter hostility, the principal invites her to unload her aggression in the more appropriate space of a private office.

Curt words hissed through tight lips relate the tale of disappointment she feels because her daughter has not been selected as a senior leader. Susan's mother angrily holds the principal responsible for not ensuring that her daughter was selected. She berates the other students chosen for senior leadership positions, telling the principal that he doesn't know what type of people his students are. According to Mrs Jones, in the run-up to the leadership selections her Susan had done all the work.

'I should know,' she says belligerently. 'I painted as many of the backdrops as I could. I was there and saw how the students worked. I know exactly who did and who did not contribute.' She suggests that the system is flawed. The principal tells her all selection systems are flawed.

Ironically, the project to which the mother refers is often overtaken by parents and reveals which students can work without parental interference. This is not to say no assistance is allowed – it is often a special time for parents and their offspring to work together – but parents should be guided by their adolescents on how deeply to become involved in projects where the students have to show their initiative.

Completely unaware of how her daughter performs against her peers, Susan's mother continues her angry tirade against the school and other students. Susan is a lovely young woman, but she is young for her class and this plays itself out at times of stress. The principal bravely tries to explain that Susan is not beyond reproach and that she has flaws that have prevented her from being selected as a leader. Demanding clarification, Susan's mother is not prepared to accept that teachers complain about Susan's immature behaviour, general lack of commitment to projects and whining negativity. The other students have witnessed her behaviour and have responded to it from time to time. Their votes suggest that they do not value Susan as a leader. Susan's mother will have none of it – after all it is her daughter and she knows her best.

The principal asks the mother if she would like to see the votes, but the mother, suddenly afraid of the truth, does not want to see evidence of what she now terms her daughter's failure.

Both mother and daughter are directed for counselling, but the disappointment is lasting and sad since the daughter perceives the situation as a disappointment not so much for herself but for her mother. This feeling is problematic for the relationship going into the future.

Disappointment is as normal to living as is breathing and yet as parents we try desperately to shield our children from disappointment. We look for excuses rather than reasons when our adolescents do not achieve what we want them to achieve. Many parents lose their dignity and minimise the value of their adolescents through their inability to manage their own disappointment in a mature and successful manner. Ironically, if managed effectively, disappointment can be a valuable teacher.

As adults we must be careful that we do not equate achievement with getting what we want. Susan's mother was unable to separate which emotions belonged to her and which emotions belonged to her daughter. When emotions feel muddled, parents will be unable to listen clearly or remain adult in order to guide their adolescent.

In another school a similar story plays itself out, only this time the consequences of the parents' disappointment are more disastrous for the adolescent's long-term career plans.

Paul, a rather suave young man nearing the end of adolescence, has been involved in some excellent community service projects and has contributed positively to the school, although the teachers have become aware of his frequent absences, particularly on Monday mornings. Recent months have seen him distracted and self-absorbed. His sallow skin looks sallower and he sports dark, tired rings under his eyes. All attempts by the school to engage with him or his parents on his behaviour and about his tiredness are fobbed off as unnecessary interference from the school. Although he is a good student academically, he has stopped participating in sport because it interferes with his scintillatingly social weekends.

The process for selecting members for the Learner Representative Council begins in earnest and Paul is keen to be selected. He feels that his community service projects and his academic ability entitle him to a place on the council. When the votes are counted, Paul receives very few votes from his peers.

Devastated at not being appointed to the council, he and his father decided to confront the headmaster and demand an explanation.

In the grey formality of the headmaster's office, Paul's mature face and stylish haircut do little to help him appear suave and sophisticated when he demands to know the reason for not having been selected to the Learner Representative Council. Both he and his father, who is blustering with anger, blame the school for Paul's failure to get a position on the council.

In order to cope with his disappointment, Paul petulantly avows to put himself first and the school can 'go to hell' as far as he and his father are concerned. When it is suggested to Paul by the headmaster that his friends feel excluded from his life because he has given up sport to engage in a serious relationship, he refuses to acknowledge his part in causing his peers to react in the way that they did. When challenged about his frequent absences, Paul says that they are being overstated and exaggerated.

Paul's father, a tall, arrogant but dapper man, insists that the other students are simply jealous of Paul's style and his maturity. Neither father nor son is prepared to acknowledge responsibility for the circumstances in which Paul finds himself. The father spits out epithets against the school, calling into question its values and integrity. Realising that he is fighting strong feelings rather than thought through concepts, the headmaster declines to escalate the conflict and he lets the father and son leave his office angry and determined to take revenge.

Paul, encouraged by his father, decides to dismiss anything for which the school stands and in so doing he compromises his academic progress considerably. By the end of his final year at school he has resorted to cheating in tests and compromising his integrity significantly. During the revision week prior to his final public examinations, he refuses to attend school and, with his father's collusion, he attends a bartender's course!

Both Paul and his father's actions are filled with a childish petulance; both father and son feel that they are punishing the school. Ironically, their actions prove that the choice made by his peers had indeed been the correct one. Through his misguided reaction to his disappointment, his immediate academic future is compromised. Paul, an intelligent, talented and academically capable young man, fails to gain early entry to a tertiary faculty of his choice. In addition, there is little for the headmaster to write on his letter of reference for Paul when he leaves the school. Most significantly, he has wasted a potentially rewarding experience of growth.

'Waitings which ripen hopes are not delays', to quote Edward Benlowes, but our instant-gratification society is not always able to value the perceived disappointment of delayed achievement. Parents who live vicariously through their children and who want reward for their parenting often seek affirmation through their children's achievements. The result is mostly disastrous.

DEVELOPMENTAL CONSIDERATIONS AND SUGGESTIONS

Mirroring, as indicated in the case studies, is more common than generally perceived since it is not often discussed or often understood by adults. The phenomenon is common because parents instinctively want to protect their offspring.

In infancy, the mother often acts as a mirror. For example, if a baby smiles at its mother, the mother, through her facial expression, tone of voice and words, reflects back the smile and so conveys the loving feelings that the baby feels and expresses through the smile. The reflection back from the mother helps the baby to validate and identify its own feelings. The baby thus begins to gain an understanding about feelings. If the baby's smile is not reciprocated by the caregiver, the baby's understanding of the emotion is compromised. In other words, reflection is about acknowledgement. In infancy the parent acknowledges and therefore assists in developing the infant's sense of self.

During adolescence the reflection or mirroring process is more complicated. It becomes important that parents accurately acknowledge the adolescent's emotions without contaminating that acknowledgement with their own perceptions. By way of illustration, if an adolescent were to hold a mirror to their emotions, then it is their own emotions that should be reflected there, not the emotions of the parent.

Parents need to ask themselves whether they are giving their children sufficient space for them to see their own reflection. In other words, if the parents have succeeded in being a healthy mirror for the adolescent, the experience of being separate individuals, united by a family bond, will occur. Being separate means being able to differentiate between the parents' own feelings and those of their adolescent.

It can be surprisingly difficult to differentiate the two emotions from each other; therefore we encourage parents to consider their responses and their emotions carefully. Often there is an intentional or accidental collusion between the feelings of the parents and the adolescents and the identities of both become enmeshed. Parents instinctively want to save their children from pain but they cannot and should not always do so. Hard as it may seem, pain can be developmentally positive for your adolescent. (Obviously this point excludes significant external trauma.)

In the early years of childrearing, parents would have worked through separation issues with their infant. Winnicott warned that 'A mother who fits in with a baby's desires too well is not a good mother' (1958, p 215). The same can be said of adolescence.

In Case Study 7, Skye's mother is trying to be 'too good a parent'. As a parent, not wanting your adolescent to suffer in *any* conceivable way may be because you find that your own pain, when reflected in your adolescent, is too unbearable. When the parent's pain is felt so keenly it is not only the pain of empathy that the parent is feeling, but a pain as though the parent himself or herself was being injured. If this occurs parents have not differentiated their feelings from the feelings of their adolescent and they are therefore overidentifying with the adolescent. Indeed, Winnicott believed that parents who were self-effacing and eager to please their children were repressing their own inner hostility.

If, as a parent, you feel angry or disempowered when your adolescent is in a difficult situation or is disappointed, you need to think about separating your own feelings, experiences and history from that of your adolescent so that you let them take responsibility for their own living.

Further, think about what your collusive behaviour may mean within you. For example, if as a child or adolescent you were not allowed to express your thoughts or emotions fully and had to merge your feelings and ideas with the opinions of others, you may consider the need to revisit and heal this part of yourself.

Failure to separate effectively results in acting out, as the parents represented in the case studies did. In the case of Skye, it was necessary for the school to set boundaries for Skye's well-being and academic progress. Skye's mother, for reasons of her own, could neither set nor understand the need for suitable boundaries. When appropriate mirroring occurs, one will have internal boundaries that prevent one's own emotions spilling over into the emotions of another. If one does not have the relevant internal boundaries, one will experience many external, and usually uncomfortable, boundaries being imposed. In the case of Skye, the school placed an external boundary on Skye's mother. Had she behaved appropriately, the external boundary would not have been required, nor would the interaction have been negative. Skye needed to have the boundaries set down by the school, but her mother's acting out of her own emotions fails Skye. Through her mother's actions Skye was denied the opportunity of experiencing her own ability to deal with choices and consequences. The same can be said of the other cases.

If you find yourself acting in a similar way to Skye's mother, question what happened in the early separation process between you and your child and then compare that to the context in which you find yourself acting out your emotions in the present. Perhaps you are being too good a parent and accidentally preventing an important learning experience from taking place. Parents can also ask themselves whether they experience their adolescent's pain as if it were happening to them, even though they are the adult in the situation. The answer to this question can help you separate which feelings belong to the adolescent and which belong to you, the parent.

Thabo, in Case Study 8, highlights complex issues, including carrying the burden of his parents' dreams on his back. Adolescents need to learn that there are consequences to the choices that they make and that poor choices can impact their lives negatively for a long time. In Thabo's case there could be legal ramifications for breaking the law.

We are interested, however, in the emotional situation that sometimes causes certain behaviour to manifest itself. Parents need to try to separate the behaviour of their adolescent from the adolescent himself, although the behaviour may be unacceptable and must be dealt with. More important though, is to remember that underpinning the aberrant behaviour is most often a message that the adolescent is trying to communicate to you. The inappropriate behaviour usually exists because the adolescent is not yet able to articulate his or her underlying need. Consider, for example, an adolescent screaming, 'I am 18 now and I can do what I like!' The screaming is not appropriate but the underlying message suggests that the adolescent needs personal space and is one that requires the parent to reflect upon and consider ways in which their attitude may need to alter.

South African society is in transition and transformation has taken slow, plodding steps. There are excellent programmes to begin to redress the wrongs of the past, but all of our troubled society needs to listen to and reflect on the voices of the adolescents trying to make sense of the disturbed and dysfunctional world that adults have bequeathed them. Adults must teach what is right and Thabo needs to embrace appropriate behaviour, yet he also needs to be understood and helped into a meaningful understanding of his own identity in a complicated context. If he can integrate his two worlds successfully and sensitively, Thabo will indeed be a future role model for right behaviour. Society, or people who constitute that society, are not beyond reproach. Society as a whole needs to acknowledge this responsibility and not shrug it off as a problem belonging to the past. As adults we are responsible for helping young people move forward effectively. It is easy to lay blame, chastise and ignore; it is more courageous and more appropriate that society engages in reflective action to allow significant change to happen within individuals and society at large. As adults we are reminded that the behaviour is often a reaction to other deep-seated emotions that require expression.

In Case Study 9, Susan's mother displays very aggressive thoughts and emotions as a defence against the extreme pain of her daughter's perceived failure to achieve. She is unable to tolerate and integrate these unwanted emotions, which belong to her alone, and she projects them into the other adolescent leaders. Engaging in a frank and adult discussion where she could acknowledge the reality that her daughter is chronologically and emotionally behind her peers, which naturally created less chance for leadership, is not allowed by the mother. She would need counselling to address her inability to separate her pain from the pain her daughter was feeling.

Reflect on the extent to which your discipline process assists your adolescent towards becoming a responsible and trustworthy adult. Being consistent in your discipline benefits your adolescent, since they will be able to pre-empt your reactions and make informed choices. In cases similar to that of Skye, the parent's behaviour could lead the adolescent to reject the parent because deep down the adolescent would know that the mother is not, in fact, reacting to her adolescent's issues but rather to unresolved issues harboured by the mother. Through the mother's inappropriate behaviour, Skye is placed in a conflict situation because if she sides with the mother and negates the school's recommendation, she will be in conflict with the school. If she sides with the school she will be in conflict with her mother. Either way it puts Skye in an impossible situation. The school will be aware of Skye's need to learn and the parent needs to respect the relationship between the school and the adolescent.

In addition, try to trust your choice of school. If you feel concerned about your adolescent, and you have considered the issues carefully, you are entitled to approach the school to discuss your concern. By no means are schools beyond reproach. Schools sometimes make mistakes around the selection of students into leadership opportunities, when awards are made or when selections for teams are made. Parents can approach the school or they can work through the perceived rejection by talking through it and reflecting on the disappointment with their adolescent. If the achievement meant a great deal to the adolescent and they have been denied an opportunity for unfair reasons, it may be necessary to seek external help to deal with the disappointment. There is nothing wrong with feeling disappointed, it is a legitimate emotion; however, the manner in which the emotion is managed is crucial.

Disappointment is part of life. We have all set our hearts at one time or another on a perfect day to grace a special occasion. None of us imagines a special occasion, for example, in the pouring rain. If the rain chooses to pour on that special day, there is no point at ranting at the reality; it is far more beneficial to make the most of the given situation than to succumb to the disappointment.

When Shakespeare's King Lear rants against the storm yelling: 'Blow, winds, and crack your cheeks! rage, blow! / You cataracts and hurricanoes, spout" (III.ii.1–2), he ignores the Fool's advice to find shelter and embraces the lessons inherent in the power of the storm. The lightning, while frightening, also serves to shed light on the landscape. So, too, parents can interpret the messages from the storms of life for their adolescents. They can allow the lightning to be illuminating and to serve as a guide, or they can reject it and allow their adolescent to succumb to the ravages of the storm.

Like the sometimes frightening but beneficial elements of a storm, so there are benefits of having conflict, anger and hate in adolescent development. As adults we need to balance the encouragement of being a sensitive and responsive parent with our desire to ameliorate and fix all negative experiences. By providing a space for reflection of the painful event, a parent can mitigate the hurt the adolescent may be feeling by allowing them to reflect on the area of pain and make it a successful learning experience. This means having a balance of adolescent experience between satisfaction and frustration. It is the experience of successfully repairing and resolving frustration and conflict that ultimately helps an adolescent move towards adulthood effectively.

SUMMING UP

- Think about how you respond to your loved ones and evaluate your listening (and mirroring) as to whether it is reflective of the other person's identity or your own.

- Achievement is not synonymous with getting your own way – disappointment is a valuable teacher.

- Healthy mirroring requires life-long practice, energy and patience.

- Mirrors have boundaries (frames). Do not be afraid of internal and external boundaries because appropriate boundaries keep us all on track.

- Parents should avoid seeking affirmation of their parenting through the achievements of their children.

4

APRIL

PEER RELATIONSHIPS AND PEER ABUSE

Peer relationships are critical to the development of the adolescent. The need for friends and the fantasy that exists around best friends are important for the parent to understand. This chapter explores how walking alongside your adolescent through the joy and pain of friendship will help the adolescent develop positive future relationships.

THE LEAVES HAVE STARTED to turn and the weather is unpredictable: hot one moment and cold the next. Carried on the breeze is the hint of winter and the reminder that there is an inherent coldness to life from time to time. Summer is fading and some moods are beginning to dip, while others are buoyed by the hope of the April holidays. The icy breeze caused by the bully is sharp and piercing. It is the coldness of cruelty against which no warm clothes can protect the emerging psyche. The coldness of rejection by the adolescent's friends, or those that are perceived to be friends, is a harsh rejection to bear during the process of defining the self.

CASE STUDY 11: BULLYING AND EFFECTIVE RESTORATION OF POWER BALANCES

George is little, wiry and smart for his age. In order to create better academic opportunities for their son, George's parents have chosen to move him to a new school in his Grade 9 year. The usual settling-in anxieties beset George but he manages to overcome them quite comfortably and is soon able to tell his parents that the move to a different school has been a good one. They are delighted with his school report and pat themselves on the back for moving their wonderful son.

Nine months after the move, their happiness is cut short. An older boy, sporting the odd proud spot of stubble, has started to call George insulting names. A social networking profile has been created in George's name and from this profile it is presumed that George has been sending hateful, violent and intolerant messages to his peers.

Although George has confided in his parents, he begs them not to react towards the perpetrator. George, mature for his age and astute, keeps questioning whether he has done something to incur the anger of the adolescent who is treating him so cruelly. The situation is abusive because it is regular, ongoing and cruel harassment. George changes his route between classes and hides himself at break time so that he does not have to confront the bully.

George's parents, angered and feeling helpless, seek both legal and psychological advice to help their son. It is decided that George should try to engage with the bully. Predictably, this attempt fails and poor George is subjected to more harassment. The parents have no alternative but to step in but they make it clear from the outset that they want to resolve the issue for their son rather than condemn the bully. The parents, although they deeply resent their son's bully, behave like adults in the situation and contain their own angry emotions. Mediation takes place between the bully, the head of the school, George and the parents. The bully is given the opportunity to apologise and George is given the opportunity to forgive him. George requests that no action be taken against the bully and the situation resolves itself favourably with no residual aftermath. (The school sets interventions in place but these are not discussed with George and his parents.)

George has learnt a great deal about himself and in particular that his physique makes him present himself as fearful and inadequate. He resolves this attitude. The positive parenting displayed by George's parents results in emotional growth for their son. Even though they are angry with the perpetrator, they know their task is to stand alongside George to resolve the problem rather than to react on his behalf.

CASE STUDY 12: WHEN FRIENDSHIPS BECOME UNKIND – A CRUEL CASE OF BULLYING

Clever, hard-working Erin is an ordinary 15 year old. Naive, kind and recently aware of her attractiveness to the opposite sex, Erin is deeply hurt to find herself suddenly isolated from her friendship group. Erin walks into the classroom and sees that her friends have moved from their usual seats and not kept her one. She brushes it off as an oversight. When she answers a question her friends roll their eyes and pass nasty, knowing looks amongst themselves. Again Erin tries to shrug their actions off and blames herself for being too sensitive. Unperceived by teachers, these actions by her so-called friends persist. They grind her down and she begins to lose weight and seeks solace in her boyfriend. She tells no one about the subtle bullying except a friend from her first year at high school, whom she had ironically rejected for the new friends.

The meanness of the girls continues, undetected by anyone because it is so insidious. Erin becomes thinner and thinner. She is too embarrassed to tell her parents and her teachers about how she feels in case 'she is being too sensitive'. Her usually excellent grades begin to decline and one of the teachers becomes aware of her withdrawal. Erin will not open up to the teacher and the teacher alerts the school counsellor, who tentatively begins to open channels of communication with Erin. No one, however, has bargained on the intensity of the emotions about to be unleashed on the gentle, kind, quiet and shy adolescent.

It is the day before the long weekend. Erin is looking forward to some respite from her tormentors for four full days. Assembly gathers students together to start the day. It is a Thursday, a day full of the hope that the long weekend promises. Erin decides to sit with her old friend and move away from the group who are victimising her. She is wisely following the advice of the school counsellor. As she sits down, unfortunately immediately behind her 'friends', they turn to look at her and begin to hiss. It is as subtle as a snake terrorising its prey and this cruelty is only observed by the friend beside her. The tears well up and Erin feels utterly humiliated and unable to concentrate in class for the rest of the day. What will her tormentors think to do next?

School closes early for the long weekend and Erin thinks she will be able to use the time to sort out her problems and tell her parents, as the school counsellor has advised her to do. But late that night her mobile phone beeps her to attention and its inbox holds a cruel message: 'Make sure your boyfriend isn't in any photos with us – his huge nose is too disgusting for us to look at.' The text burns into Erin and she feels angry and exhausted by the taunting.

While the message may seem marginally hurtful but ridiculous to an adult, it is overwhelming for Erin. There is no point in continuing to fight the world that is so mean. Her parents are asleep and she does not want to disturb them. She goes to the bathroom cabinet and takes whatever pain medication there is to take. She swallows it all. It is past midnight when she texts the friend she has once rejected and tells her what she has done.

With huge courage and a deep sense of the urgency of the circumstances, the once-discarded friend contacts a senior member of the school staff. The staff member contacts the parents and urges them to get Erin to hospital.

Now aware of the full extent of the situation, the senior member of the school staff and the school counsellor address Erin's situation. The consequences of the peer abuse could have been fatal.

Erin does not recover immediately but the bullying stops because the bullies are dealt with very severely. Erin requires therapeutic intervention and she is equipped with coping strategies to develop assertiveness.

DEVELOPMENTAL CONSIDERATIONS AND SUGGESTIONS

Adolescents *really* believe that their parents know very little. Good parents have given their adolescents appropriate space to challenge them in order to start separating into independent young adults. Having given the adolescent the opportunity to separate, friends become very important to the adolescent. The 'all-knowing' friend is very often the barometer for how adolescents are feeling, thinking and what they are doing. Adolescents will have taken with them that which the parents have modelled to them since infancy and it is this understanding of relationships that they are most likely to take into their future relationships.

By and large, adolescence is a time for parents to let their adolescents get on with friendships while remaining in the wings for the parts of friendship that are stormy. Parents would do well to remember that certain types of conflict that occur within friendships provide excellent opportunities for the adolescent to develop resilience. In the short term the pain of conflict could feel immense, but in the long term the adolescent may use the opportunity to begin to develop useful conflict-resolution skills.

Remember that since the adolescent personality is fluid, so too may relationships be less stable than relationships in adulthood. Girls sometimes fantasise about having a very close friendship with another girl where secrets are shared and company is enjoyed. These friendships can happen but can also be fairly volatile. As personalities shift, so do friendships and it may be useful to point out to girls that these perfect friendships may be less perfect than they seem. Girls tend to be exclusionary in their friendships, while boys operate friendships within groups. Interestingly, research shows that, unlike boys, there is no significant need among girls to break familial bonds. Boys, because they are more comfortable to separate from existing bonds, tend to be less anxious about friendship. Generally boys can be more frank in their communication while girls in the early stages of adolescence are afraid to express themselves authentically.

Parents may struggle to walk alongside their adolescent's friendships and many parents want to barge right into the adolescent relationship. Parents who text-message their adolescent's friends or involve themselves in minor adolescent conflicts are most likely mirroring inappropriately. Obviously if the conflict moves to a level of abuse the parent must step in immediately. In other words, it is important for the parent to be available to ease the heartache but not to intervene and take sides, since culpability for misunderstandings in friendship issues is difficult to place. Generally adolescents want their parents to hear and listen to their pain but they do not necessarily want the parent to rescue them.

Rachel Simmons, author of *Odd Girl Out*, talks about there being unwritten rules in friendships, particularly with girls, and these rules can often get adolescents into trouble. For example, girls can be loyal to each other even if loyalty means despising a girl that they in fact like because the most powerful adolescent in the group demands negative, unkind behaviour from them.

Adolescents sometimes lose themselves and develop a false identity to cope within a given group. Regardless of how destructive and terrible this false identity may be, it is constructed in order to fit in. As adolescents mature they should be able to discard and refuse behaviour that is not congruent with their own personal self or their values. In time, they should become aware that insulting or excluding a fellow human being is unacceptable. Should positive integration of values within their behaviour not occur, the parent should attempt to guide their adolescent towards an understanding of their true self that has become compromised. Parents could have a valuable and philosophical debate with their adolescents around the meaning of friendship and how blind loyalty for the sake of belonging is dangerous for the development not only of an individual but also for society.

As parents, it is our duty to help our adolescents establish appropriate rules of decency so that they can value fellow human beings. Friends should bring out the best in each other and adolescents could be challenged about how their friends bring the best out in them and how they, in turn, bring out the best in their friends. Peers that encourage each other to engage in dangerous or negative behaviour are not friends.

When noticing that their adolescents are being unkind to others, parents should try to separate the frustrated emotion from the actual cruel behaviour. Debate the emotion without denying its existence but be clear to show the adolescent that the behaviour is unacceptable. For example, if your adolescent mimics sarcastically with other friends a peer's incessant questioning in class, acknowledge that you know your adolescent feels frustrated with the time that the questioning takes, leaving little time for the teacher to actually teach. The cruel mocking behaviour can be identified, thus teaching your adolescent that the behaviour helps no one and if anything is destructive.

A valuable question for a parent to ask is whether there is a link between events the adolescent is experiencing in the relationships with events happening at home. It may be valuable to assess whether relationships, including that of the parents, is conflictual or harmonious or whether one partner is significantly more domineering (bullying) than the other. Assess whether people in the home environment give space to each other so that good listening occurs. Serious conflicts within peer relationships very rarely come out of the blue and invariably they reflect aspects of another relationship.

Victims of bullying need space to express their trauma. In Erin's case she resorted to attempted suicide in order to get attention. To avoid high levels of trauma, it is important to notice behavioural changes in your adolescent. Unexplained fluctuations in weight, marks or grades, personality and behaviour are usually indicators of distress in an adolescent. Erin clearly had underlying inadequacy issues that needed to be addressed and obviously the girls bullying her needed to be stopped in their tracks.

In George's case, he had a healthier sense of self and supportive parents. This combination allowed for significant positive growth to occur. Erin's parents needed support in their parenting of Erin since they needed to establish more open, less fearful lines of communication with their daughter.

In some instances, peer relationship problems can indicate sibling rivalry. Sibling issues may be the cause if an adolescent cannot tolerate sharing friends with others, worries that they will lose their friends to others, or does not feel satisfied in a group unless he or she is the centre of attention.

Occasionally an adolescent's position within the family may impact friendships. An eldest child may feel comfortable leading peer groups, while a middle child could develop a tendency to feel lost and without an identity in a group. Youngest children may wish to be spoilt by their peers since they have had their needs easily met by older siblings. Only children sometimes feel neglected by their peers since they experience the respect that is often afforded the elder sibling by the parents and the spoiling that sometimes attends the younger sibling. If an only child has not had the opportunity to share with other children, they may struggle to allow peers to have things first in the friendship.

If an adolescent is jealous of another adolescent, parents need to think about how they have treated this adolescent in relation to another sibling. It may be that the adolescent is inherently envious of others or they may have perceived that the parent finds them less lovable than the other siblings. You may want to ask whether you found the adolescent, as an infant, to be a difficult child, to be unpleasant or perhaps there was inadequate bonding. Alternatively, if adolescents have been indulged by their parents, they will probably demand similar indulgence from their peers.

Helping your adolescent make the links to their roles and experiences at home and how this translates into their current friendships may help them be more flexible in their role within a friendship group.

While we have unpacked what may lie beneath some behaviour in friendships, we want to stress that bullying or peer abuse is serious. Peer abuse or bullying can be said to take place when harassment is regular and ongoing and it is usually cruel. If you are concerned that your child is being bullied, or is a bully, you should not hesitate to ask the school for help.

Peer abuse should not be confused with teasing and joking, but if your adolescent's development is compromised by the actions of a peer or a bullying teacher, adult intervention is urgent and necessary. The consequences of bullying behaviour can be long term and dire if not dealt with adequately and professional therapeutic intervention may be important. Good schools are aware that bullying occurs, but they may need to be alerted to specific instances. Peer abuse in the twenty-first century has become complicated by social networking technologies and it is a phenomenon that must be managed rather than ignored.

Peer abuse is unacceptable and both the victims and the perpetrators need to be supported to avoid long-term emotional damage.

SUMMING UP

- Encourage a move away from dependence on parents and provide space for adolescents to move toward meaningful peer friendships.

- Some conflict in friendships can provide opportunities to develop resilience. If the conflict moves to a level of abuse, step in immediately.

- Evaluate relationships between members of the family at home to see whether unhealthy modelling is taking place.

- In a true friendship both parties bring out and seek the best in each other.

- Abuse or bullying occurs when harassment is ongoing, repeated and nasty. It should not be tolerated.

- As a general rule, parents should not get involved in adolescent squabbles and should respect the privacy of the adolescent.

5

MAY

'ACTING OUT' VERSUS 'THINKING THROUGH': SEX, DRUGS AND ROCK AND ROLL

In their desire to be in control and adultlike, adolescents 'act out' rather than 'think through' their behaviour. Understanding the concept of acting out can help parents fathom, while not necessarily condone, the sometimes incomprehensible actions of adolescents. This chapter looks at certain behaviour that concerns parents and offers some explanations.

MAY IS A MONTH that is neither here nor there: it is neither hot nor cold. Summer has gone and winter is soon to be upon us. The rich colours of the autumn leaves are lovely, but they are also the harbingers of some difficult times. May is a typically adolescent month: it's summer one day and winter the next. Just as May is betwixt and between, so adolescents don't quite know where they are and they resort to acting on impulse rather than thinking through, because they are neither child nor adult. Some of their emotions reflect the high days of summer, while others reflect the loneliness inherent in winter.

CASE STUDY 13: ACTING OUT TO DISSIPATE BOREDOM

The group is disgruntled – they want to be finished with school. Sustaining their energy for anything beyond the absolute bare necessities of their academic endeavours feels impossible. To allay their boredom and add something different to the incessant ennui of waiting to finish Grade 12, some members of the group conjure a plan. They invent a competition to see how many times they can bunk a particular non-academic lesson. They notch up their successes by drawing a line on a chosen wall of a little storeroom, where they hide themselves from the offending drag of the day. The 50 minutes hidden in a poky room is infinitely longer than 50 minutes in a classroom, but the challenge of who can notch up the most 'bunking lines' compels them and provides them with a weekly entertainment slot, while also giving them the opportunity to plug their music into their ears and transport themselves to other dreamy worlds of love and idealism.

CASE STUDY 14: ACTING OUT AS ATTENTION-SEEKING BEHAVIOUR

Maggie is desperately unhappy. Mom and Dad have divorced and she detests the new relationships she has to endure. Her head wants to split in agony. Everything is awful and she desperately wants someone to notice her. She makes up stories in an attempt to get sympathy. She exaggerates the troubled home situation and develops fictitious illnesses and bandages imaginary wounds.

Her friends grow wary and weary of her deceptions and then one day in the middle of the school day, Maggie disappears. She is nowhere to be found. A teacher has noticed that she is not in her lesson. Attendance records and accounts from peers indicate she was indeed at school. Calls to her cellphone are not answered. The usual hiding places for the habitual bunkers are checked. Maggie is nowhere. Desperate messages are left on her phone. The security guards insist they have not seen any student leave the school premises. When her mother is called to see if she has collected her daughter from school unusually early, her answer of 'no' turns to rage. 'You have lost my daughter,' she yells, holding the school fully accountable for her daughter's actions. Her mother's calls to Maggie's cellphone are also left unanswered.

The principal leaves a message on Maggie's cellphone to say that they are about to call in the police as they are deeply concerned about her whereabouts. The message is obviously retrieved by Maggie, who sheepishly emerges as if from nowhere. Tears stream down her face. They are tears of joy and pain: tears of joy because she knows people were concerned for her and had noticed her absence; tears of sadness because she has to resort to distressing tactics to get attention.

CASE STUDY 15: DANGEROUS ACTING OUT

A small group of Grade 10s regularly bunk three consecutive lessons every Wednesday. They are a motley, dishevelled group of boys and girls whose bunking escapade starts rather innocently but ends in a very different place.

The first Wednesday, one student, not having done his homework, begs his friend James to go with him to his girlfriend's house close to the school. A few hangers on join the two and they giggle their way out of an unguarded back gate of the school.

The little group drink coffee, listen to music and chat. Before they know it they have missed three lessons. They sidle back to school and realise with a sense of misplaced pride that no one has noticed their absence. And so begins a little Wednesday bunking ritual, initially harmless save for the wasted academic time. But joking and speaking inanities soon become as boring as school, until James introduces a little marijuana to the group. Suddenly the Wednesday bunking group takes on a new dimension.

The group's escapades are discovered after a great deal of damage has been done. One of the girls falls pregnant and during one of the Wednesday sessions the group plans to arrange an abortion for her. From planning false phone calls to parents to creating elaborate excuses for their being away from school for an extended period, they think they have the problem solved. Their sense of supremacy allows them to feel that they can organise and handle anything, but they do not have the capacity to think through the consequences of their actions.

Only at this dangerous point does Emily, one of the girls who has been caught up in the Wednesday game, begin to think about consequences. Unable to cope with the deceit and fearful of what might happen to her friend, Emily has the courage to seek the help of an adult she trusts. Unlike her peers, she is thinking ahead. It has taken a crisis for one reasonable adolescent to realise that their actions are becoming out of control. Hard as it is for her, Emily decides to expose the Wednesday rituals, which have become dangerous and disturbed.

DEVELOPMENTAL CONSIDERATIONS AND SUGGESTIONS

The term 'acting out' is used to describe the thoughtless activity often engaged in by adolescents as an attempt to recapture the sense of supremacy that they felt in childhood and that they feel they have lost in adolescence. Simply put, acting out means that adolescents act first rather than thinking first and then acting in a considered way. While acting-out-type behaviour never completely leaves us, mature adults usually try to integrate their thoughts with who they are, rather than acting on their more wild thoughts and fantasies.

During adolescence most acting out behaviour, while annoying for adults, is perfectly normal. Adults, and particularly schools, have a tendency to overreact to harmless examples of acting out because they fear for the safety of the adolescent. Adolescents have to try out different personas from time to time in order to know what aspects to integrate into their core personality. While adolescents are acting out these personas, we say that their personalities are *fluid* because some of the meaning behind the behaviour will in fact be incorporated into what will become their adult personality. To deny them the opportunity to act out safely is to deny them appropriate progress towards a more stable personality for adulthood.

It is important to distinguish ordinary acting out that is appropriate from destructive and unhealthy acting out. For example, it is normal for an adolescent to want attention and therefore attention-seeking behaviour is typical. In Case Study 13 – that of the disgruntled Grade 12s – the act of bunking indicates relatively healthy acting out. Case Study 14 – that of Maggie who 'disappears' – points to excessive acting out owing to the underlying desperate emotion that drives the behaviour, while the acting out in Case Study 15 – the group of Grade 10s who bunk out weekly – is compounded by the frequency of the bunking, which then leads to additional dangerous acting out.

The frequency of acting out is often an indicator of significant underlying issues that need to be managed. Aspects of Case Study 15 will be addressed throughout this chapter. As adults we need to explore and differentiate between which actions help the adolescent develop as a person and those which do not.

Adolescents will experiment and with this comes some acting out that is appropriate and helpful. Acting out is common behaviour because adolescents are often impulsive and not yet mature. Many of the cases in this book, for example, reflect an element of acting out. The behaviour sometimes helps in the developmental process towards maturity. Parents need to understand the acting out and to help their adolescents think through their actions when, because of immaturity, they cannot. For example, adolescents may lie about minor issues where they are dealing with an immaturity in themselves. If, for instance, they cannot own up to talking to a member of the opposite sex, they are acting out because of their shyness; they are not necessarily being intentionally deceitful.

While it is difficult, try to understand the motivation behind the adolescent's acting out. It may be helpful to recall your own adolescent experiences when trying to fathom the actions of your adolescent. Extreme or excessive behaviour is inappropriate acting out. We hope to offer parents some guidelines as to how to understand the meaning of the behaviour, what the adolescent may be experiencing and how to help them. First, it is helpful to identify the healthiness of the behaviour that may at first glance appear aberrant.

Acting out can become destructive and socially inappropriate for adolescents when, for example, they bully and hurt their peers significantly. The behaviour is usually gendered. Boys will hit each other to affirm their masculinity, while girls will use exclusionary tactics to elevate their status in a group. Neither male nor female adolescents will necessarily think through their chosen behaviour. Certain acting out behaviour, such as cutting, substance abuse and attempted suicide, requires professional help.

With the development of modern society, improved theoretical and clinical knowledge of adolescents' needs, and seemingly more difficult behaviour, such as suicidal tendencies and cutting or self-mutilating, parents have adapted their parenting styles. For example, parents are being more active than in years gone by in helping their adolescents with their emotions and trying to support them in their vulnerability. There has been a marked increase in the number of parents seeking advice in the parent-adolescent dyad because the consequences of not doing so are markedly more severe than in previous generations.

Imagine the concept of acting out on a continuum. On the healthy side are those adolescents who are sometimes rude to their friends, express melodramatic emotions or outrageous thoughts. When they start thinking about their behaviour, it usually stops after a little while and often leaves the adolescent feeling embarrassed, because when they try to integrate this behaviour into their identity, they see the discrepancies between their behaviour and their values. Stopping the acting out usually occurs only when adolescents are forced to think about their behaviour, so parents and other adults can encourage adolescents to think about their actions. Noting and understanding the dissonance that occurs between behaviour and values is immensely valuable in the growing-up process because the adolescent may, through reflection on their behaviour, decide that they are not the person the behaviour might suggest and that they do not want to be associated with or labelled according to the acting out behaviour.

Sometimes it helps for the adolescent to experience being slightly out of control in order to learn from the experience and therefore not to want to return to that feeling again. Obviously frequent occurrences of being out of control, albeit mildly, do not fit onto the healthy side of the continuum.

The problem with acting out arises when behaviour is at the extreme end of the continuum, as suggested in Case Study 15 where the acting out becomes dangerous. Adolescent behaviour becomes extreme when, for example, adolescents are violent or extremely aggressive rather than rude, or harm their bodies physically by ingesting dangerous substances, or if they self mutilate. In cases of extreme acting out, the adolescents have literally cut off the emotion they are feeling or the thought they are thinking. They have lost control of good thinking ability.

You will see in the case studies that at first the adolescents *genuinely* do not know the reason for their behaviour because they truly have disconnected their thinking from their emotion. Continuing with the behaviour no longer helps the adolescent to grow up because their thinking is no longer working to help them learn from the real consequences of their behaviour. Neither do they learn to understand the meaning of the emotions that they are feeling and that may be prompting their behaviour.

Parents who mitigate the real consequences of poor choices made by adolescents can negatively impede their progress into mature and appropriately responsible young adults. For example, in Case Study 14 Maggie's mother is angry with the school but fails to acknowledge that her daughter has acted inappropriately and thoughtlessly.

Adolescents, in the immediate moment of destructive behaviour, do not see themselves as emotionally unwell or in need because they are detached from themselves and their actions. It is usually parents and friends who become concerned. It can be very frightening for another adolescent, and even an adult, to hear or see someone out of control or engaging in harmful or potentially life-threatening behaviour. Deep down the disturbed adolescent who is acting out will be aware of an extreme anxiety or aggression that desperately needs to be channelled.

Parents need to help adolescents find a way to connect emotionally in a way that reflects a 'thinking through' process as opposed to an 'acting out' process. Since this book deals mainly with healthy adolescents, we cannot fully explain in this space the reasons that someone reaches the stage of needing to act out destructively. In all extreme cases of acting out, professional help is strongly recommended because as stated in the Introduction, adolescents do have the capacity to harm or kill themselves or others. Having identified the severity of the acting out, it is important to evaluate whether additional, professional support is needed. The safety of the adolescent must always be foremost in decisions around seeking support. When reflecting on the acting out, parents can help the adolescent by thinking about what may have led to the acting out behaviour in the first instance.

The age and frequency at which acting out begins is usually significant in determining the extent to which the actions or behaviour may be destructive. If a child begins to act out in latency (between about six and nine years) and is hostile, aggressive or excessively needy, they may have a propensity to act out in a negative and possibly dangerous way during adolescence. (Parents should be cautious not to confuse naughtiness or mischievous behaviour with inappropriate acting out.)

The weary topic of underage drinking falls into the category of inappropriate acting out. Drinking alcohol, getting drunk or abusing substances, be it as an adolescent or an adult, is a form of unhealthy acting out. Often adolescents will drink alcohol and smoke because it makes them feel more adult. They are acting out their desire to feel more grown up rather than thinking through the consequences and meaning of their actions. Often adolescents will go to a party or a club with the specific intention of getting drunk. Under the influence of alcohol they feel more confident, more outgoing and they have the misperception that they are being affirmed. Physiologically they are compromising the health of their bodies and their brains.

Most adolescents do not have the capacity to think through the consequences of their actions and need adults to set down firm boundaries for them around drinking and substances. Adolescents who get drunk frequently or who abuse substances are invariably not confident and their insecurity and underlying unhappiness requires urgent adult attention. Parents are also urged to review their own relationship with substances since they are modelling behaviour for their adolescents.

It goes without saying, and is indicated by Case Study 15 in this chapter, that abuse of substances, including alcohol, can and often does lead to inappropriate and dangerous acting out, and in particular it leads to promiscuity amongst adolescents. Physically adolescents' bodies are becoming more sexual as they move towards sexual maturity and adulthood. Boys in particular are obsessed with sex and the interest in the opposite sex often surpasses all other interests. Adolescent boys and girls will regularly dream about sex. The exploration of the body becomes common and masturbation is a normal part of the growing-up process. Adolescents need space to experience their sexual identities rather than to experience sex.

Typically adolescents may use clothes to express their burgeoning sexual identity. Normal acting out around this may present itself in flirtatious behaviour and marginally provocative dressing. Bordering on the dangerous side of the continuum would be the common behaviour of adolescents who go to parties and kiss numerous acquaintances on the same night. They would, in this case, be acting out their desire to feel extremely desirable to the opposite sex. The next day, the adolescent is likely to feel awkward, embarrassed and rather sheepish on account of their promiscuous behaviour. They will probably feel that they have let themselves down because their behaviour would in all likelihood have conflicted with their values. Thinking through their behaviour and reintegrating it more appropriately into their identity would have rendered the acting out of their emotions useful. Repeating the behaviour would indicate a lack of thought and an immaturity.

If an adolescent begins to engage in numerous sexual encounters that have no meaningful attachments, it is extremely concerning since it points to a dangerous acting out of a deep-seated unresolved need to belong in a meaningful relationship. It can also reflect an alienation from the body or an alienation from the true feelings and thoughts that lie deep inside the adolescent.

It is, however, important to note that many older adolescents who are engaging in sex are not acting out, but perceive sex to be part of a meaningful relationship. If this is the case with your adolescent, it is important to have significant conversations around contraception, values, HIV/AIDS and other sexually transmitted infections.

Music is often important to adolescents and can be an area of contention in the home. Again it is useful to remember the earlier, probably easier and younger days with your child. Most good parents will have exposed their children, while they were little, to fairy tales, folk tales and stories. One of the values of telling stories lies not only in helping children develop creativity, but also in helping with the psychological task of growing up by providing symbolic expression for their feelings. Symbolic expression suggests that children gently learn that they cannot always be supreme and that disappointment and challenge are part of life. Through this experience children can gain a sense of selfhood and self worth.

As children move into adolescence, stories are no longer one of the main avenues through which they begin to understand themselves.

Music and song lyrics begin to play an important role. Rock music, for example, has long had the reputation of representing the outsider or the person distanced from mainstream culture. The sound of alternative music, rap music or music which is loud, rhythmic and 'in your face' is suggestive of the alienation from society that adolescents often love to feel and express. Adolescents can internalise the music and relate their own feelings, be it love or hate, to the lyrics and rhythm because music often resonates with the themes close to the heart of the adolescent.

Reasonable acting out in relation to music is a healthy tool for adolescents because it is a time when they defy their parents in the process of separating from them. Music is a space for them to experience and cope with their separate identity. Listening to music that resonates with the dissonance they may be feeling can be useful in integrating these emotions of separateness. The adolescent's relationship with music is therefore healthy, up to a point. When they overidentify with the music or the performer and begin to act out on the lyrics or adopt the persona of the artist, parents need to intervene to address the unbalanced behaviour.

In Case Study 15, the influence of the peers exacerbated the negative acting out that was taking place. Parents who feel anxious about the peers with whom their adolescent has chosen to associate should monitor the relationships closely. If any behaviour is not compatible with your own family values, it is not only your right but also your responsibility to guide your adolescent towards other friendships. If adolescents have positive interactions with peers, where there is an appropriate balance of power in the relationship, they are likely to avoid dangerous acting out behaviour.

Typically adolescents who have families who do not model good relationships and who are unable to set appropriate boundaries in a loving manner will become vulnerable to delinquent acting out. The best way to deal with aberrant behaviour is to intervene early. No matter how early intervention occurs, it cannot succeed if we dedicate ourselves exclusively to treating the adolescent; the parents need to consider themselves within the context of their adolescent's behaviour. The impact of effective parenting is obvious. One of the premises of this book is that what parents do, does in fact matter.

Parents who do not allow or who forget the need for adolescents to connect from time to time with their narcissistic or supreme sense of self can emotionally shatter the adolescent because the adolescent will begin to perceive themselves as inadequate. It is often this sense of inadequacy which causes the adolescent to act out and behave antisocially.

As adolescents separate from their parents in their move towards adulthood there may be a loneliness that accompanies the process. Loneliness occurs because they are moving their primary love from their parents to new adult relationships. The concomitant emptiness is often defended by overuse of alcohol, substances, food, sex or the internet. Parents can mitigate the sense of loss and loneliness by acknowledging the emotional space the adolescent is in. Parents should walk alongside their adolescent rather than trying to fill the space caused by the loneliness, since the emotion represents an important moment of personality growth for the emerging adult.

Whenever an adolescent is acting out, parents need to remember that the adolescent is not thinking rationally or emotionally appropriately and parents can help by simply *acknowledging* the emotions being felt by the adolescent. Once these are acknowledged, together you can try to understand what part you, as a parent, played – if any at all – in your adolescent's acting out. It is also most important to reflect on the part the adolescent played. Try to understand what your adolescents are trying to communicate to you through their actions. Once you have understanding, you have a good idea of how to respond.

SUMMING UP

- Try to understand that your adolescent is trying to communicate their emotions and feelings through their actions.

- Separating the behaviour from the adolescent helps the parent to start communicating with the emotion the adolescent is really trying to express.

- Acting out is an attempt to recapture the sense of supremacy lost in childhood.

- If an adolescent talks about suicide, adults must take their talk seriously and consider the reason the adolescent is so angry.

- Adolescents need to learn that there are consequences to the choices that they make in their lives.

- Before attacking the adolescent for bad behaviour, parents need to ask whether they themselves are violent, drink too much, self medicate inappropriately, have unhealthy eating issues or display 'acting out' rather than 'thinking through' behaviour.

6

JUNE

CHOOSING SUBJECTS: WHOSE ISSUE IS IT ANYWAY?

Choosing subjects, like considering careers, is a difficult time of facing present realities and future possibilities. It is a time for coming to terms with the separate identities of adolescents and their parents and the process needs thoughtfulness, maturity and understanding. The case studies in this chapter offer very different perspectives, but both require parents to be alert and aware of their adolescents' abilities.

DAYS BEGIN AND END in biting cold and the seemingly never-ending winter term is alleviated only by the excitement around winter sports and school plays. Rugby matches provide welcome respite from the cold winter days. Hockey practices and netball matches keep students energised when their default reaction may be the desire to hibernate not only from the weather but also from the important decisions that attach themselves to winter terms. Depending on the grade, subject choices and future career decisions all have to be made or at least considered. Hard weather and hard decisions are markers for this time of year and parents are often overwhelmed by the decisions their adolescents have to make.

CASE STUDY 16: THE LIMITING EFFECTS OF AN INCORRECT SUBJECT CHOICE

After the statutory requirement subjects, a sound pass in physical science is the gateway subject to all engineering and health science qualifications. Like mathematics, it is considered a 'high stakes' subject. Parents attach importance to the subject often to the detriment of their child's future.

Karabo is a highly energetic, enthusiastic and popular pupil in Grade 9. She is loved by the school on account of her ebullience and wonderful sense of humour. Karabo is a solid student academically, a good sportswoman and a talented singer and actress. Her scintillating personality comes alive on the stage. Her leadership skills are astonishing and she can get a group on her side in no time at all.

Karabo's parents have very specific aspirations for their daughter. Their choice of school has incurred a measure of sacrifice on their part and this may add to the aspirational intensity attached to their daughter's future. These aspirations become very clear at subject choice time. Karabo wants to pursue a career in the dramatic arts. She excels in English and loves being on the stage. Mathematically she is more than competent but not exceptional. For her parents though, going into the arts is simply not an option for their daughter. She is to be a doctor and failing that, a businesswoman. They insist that she take physical science as a subject. They forbid her from selecting dramatic arts as a subject, in spite of her passion and obvious and significant talent.

Karabo chooses what her parents advise and the school's advice is ignored. Her entire selection of subjects is in the scientific band, even though these are her least favourite subjects. By the end of her Grade 11 year, Karabo is increasingly unhappy because she is putting so much effort into trying to manage the science that her extramural involvement in the dramatic arts has declined significantly. Not only this, but she is barely achieving passing grades.

Karabo's applications to universities using Grade 11 marks are severely compromised and she is certainly not going to achieve well enough to get into a health sciences faculty, let alone a top business degree. She scrapes into her final year of high school. Despite being selected to a senior leadership position and playing in the top sports teams, Karabo continues to be unhappy as she struggles with subjects that do not reflect her noteworthy linguistic and artistic strengths.

At the end of her Grade 12 year, Karabo achieves a mediocre passing grade and begins a commerce degree to appease her parents' aspirations. After three years at university, Karabo finally transfers to a dramatic arts degree, where she excels.

Her parents had compromised Karabo's happiness at school and put her in danger of failing completely, in spite of her having a superior linguistic ability.

Every year this story repeats itself and children hobble through the last few years of high school trying to fulfil their parents' wishes when they could be enjoying learning and building on their strengths.

Choosing subjects that have high status but being unable to achieve meaningfully in those subjects will severely curtail the young person's future options – indeed more so than if they had not opted for those subjects in the first instance.

CASE STUDY 17: KNOWING YOUR CHILD – WHEN TEACHERS MAKE MISTAKES

It is important to acknowledge that sometimes the advice given by teachers not to take a certain subject is well advised and in the best interests of the student. However, when it is mixed with a personal dislike for the student, then careful consideration of the teacher's motives needs to be undertaken.

Jake has always performed well academically but in his Grade 9 year he has become a little disruptive in lessons. If there is mischief in the class, Jake is usually at the centre of it. The more creative the teacher, the better able they are not only to manage Jake but also to enjoy his quirkiness.

During a science lesson, Jake takes a broom and lodges it under the handle of the door. Jake jokingly suggests that if the teacher is going to be late, she deserves to struggle to get into the lesson. The class takes great delight in observing the teacher frantically trying to open the door and then storming off in anger when she cannot budge the handle. Feeling bad at his antics, Jake goes to call the teacher and explains that it was his actions that caused the door to jam. Instead of accepting the behaviour as the young adolescent prank that it was and dealing with it quickly and cleverly, the teacher tells her colleagues about Jake's actions and they decide that Jake is a ne'er do well who will not manage the demands of their subject. From that day forward, Jake's marks fall and some of the teachers in the science department treat him poorly.

When subject choice time comes round, they inform Jake that he does not have 'the necessary discipline and fortitude' to manage science. In spite of a good mathematics mark, he is told that science will be beyond his reach.

When discussing his options with his parents, he tells them that he has been encouraged not to do science. When the parents go to discuss the matter with the science teachers, they are told that Jake does not seem to have the capabilities to do science. The parents feel that the teachers' explanations are inadequate and seek the advice of the school psychologist.

Through the use of diagnostic tests, the psychologist reveals that there is no underlying academic flaw and that Jake's non-performance in science needs greater investigation since the test suggests he should cope very well with the subject.

She asks certain questions:
- Does Jake want to take the subject?
- Are his parents pressurising him to perform, particularly in the areas of concern?
- Why are his parents disappointed by his non-performance?

The psychologist directs the parents to the school principal. Further investigations reveal that there is indeed a personality clash between Jake and two of the science teachers.

Most disconcerting is the fact that investigations show that marks have been manipulated by the teachers. The parents insist on a corrected exam paper being made available to them, from which marks have been taken and which has not been viewed by their son. Sections of the work have been marked without adherence to the memorandum. (This highlights the fact that parents should be aware of students' rights with regard to assessment protocols in schools.)

The principal is asked to solve the problem in a way that is least disruptive for the student and which will affirm his ability. However, important ground has been lost in terms of Jake's self-esteem around the subject. The parents leave the school to manage the situation, but they all agree that Jake will take science as a subject since he has both the aptitude for it and an interest in the subject.

DEVELOPMENTAL CONSIDERATIONS AND SUGGESTIONS

Many students know exactly which subjects they want to choose and the process is simple. Some schools limit the choice of subjects for financial reasons and they stream certain subjects in the same subject lines for ease of timetabling. Sometimes parents have chosen schools without giving due consideration to the subject choice limitations of a given school. It is important too for parents to understand that it is often difficult for schools to accommodate an unusual subject combination that is selected by only a few students in an entire grade.

There are many factors that need to be taken into consideration by parents, pupils and teachers when subject choices are made. It is a time for reality checks and the honesty barometer has to be set on high. It may be useful for parents to read the chapter on mirroring (Chapter 3) and understand that the subject choice made by their child is not a time for vicarious decision-making. It is a time to guide by standing alongside the child and advising and encouraging rather than dictating and insisting. Even though parents and their children can have very different abilities, it is also a time for parents to reflect upon their own abilities at high school and not make unreasonable demands on their adolescents.

Good schools are usually well versed on the requirements of the different universities and the different faculties within the universities. Schools are subject to the statutory requirements of the state and should inform parents and pupils how their marks and subject choices will determine what type of certificate will be obtained at the end of the Grade 12 year. All these factors must be borne in mind when subject choices are made.

Having to guide their adolescents through the difficulties of choosing subjects often confronts parents unexpectedly and they feel ill prepared to help their adolescent. If the parent is feeling overwhelmed, they should consult with the school or an advisor for additional advice.

An adolescent's brain is still developing and the brain usually only completes its development at about age 25. The implications of these findings suggest that we can talk about abilities of adolescents but cannot be definitive about them until they chronologically reach adulthood. In psychology too, adolescents are not meant to be diagnosed with major disorders as they are still developing physically and emotionally. These factors compound the difficulties around the choice of subjects.

Parents must be careful neither to limit their adolescent by their own limitations nor to place undue pressure on their adolescent by having unreasonable expectations. It is worthwhile to remember that some adolescents have an unhealthy desire to be perfect in order to please their parents. Adolescents can act out through academic perfection, which is usually indicative of an underlying need to be valued by the parents. Academic excellence is possible but should not be achieved at the expense of the spontaneity that attends adolescence. Naturally intelligent adolescents should be encouraged to achieve well. Parents should refrain from measuring their adolescents against the performance of other adolescents since this will significantly compromise their adolescent's self-esteem.

If a parent cannot tolerate the behaviour of the adolescent within the academic context, for example a poor work ethic, the parent should consider why they are feeling so intensely about the given issue. Depending on the answer, further thought may be needed. For example, in Case Study 16 the intention of the parents may have been good if there was anxiety around Karabo's losing out on becoming independent and secure, both financially and in a career. If Karabo's parents felt that she was capable of achieving in the scientific arena but that she was not motivated to do so, they needed to work with the school in understanding where the deficit lay. A diagnostic test is sometimes an indicator of where an individual's abilities and deficits lie. As difficult as it may be to do so, parents need to consider neurological difficulties that may impede their adolescent's academic progress.

At no point do we wish to suggest that adolescents should be exonerated from working hard to achieve reachable goals. If an adolescent is denying, and thus cutting off, a very able part of who they are, it is important to think through and discuss the meaning of their behaviour rather than reacting emotionally to it. In some circumstances it may be advisable to engage the services of a neutral person to establish the reason for the lack of motivation to achieve within a known area of capability.

Parents are entitled to feel enraged when their adolescent is lied to or is deprived of their rightful choices, as happened with Jake in Case Study 17. Adolescents can be guided to practise their assertiveness rather than becoming defensive and wanting to seek revenge at the wrongdoing of an adult. In all situations it can be good for an adolescent to look at and reflect on two questions: What belongs to me? What belongs to the other party? Perhaps in Case Study 17, Jake could rethink what his behaviour provoked in the teacher and why. At no point is the teacher's rejection or treatment of the student acceptable; if the student irritates the teacher, the teacher, as the adult, is required to rise above the situation.

While subject selection may be a trying time, it is a wonderful opportunity to listen to your adolescents and marvel at the level of thinking of which they are capable. It is a time of enjoying your adolescent as you grapple with them about their future, but remember that even though they sound adult-like, they still depend on you as parents to be consistent in your thinking and consistent with your boundaries. They need you to balance the space for them to imagine being an artist or a mathematician, but at the same time you need to be solid and reliable enough to lean on when they feel confused, lost, stupid or grandiose!

SUMMING UP

- Listen carefully to your adolescent and be realistic about options.

- Listen to the advice given by the school, but if you are confused seek further independent advice.

- Do not force your adolescent down a path that they do not want to go on, unless not doing so will compromise their future radically.

- Stand alongside your adolescent at this important time.

- Ensure that the school has made the various options clear to you. This is a time when schools and parents must work closely together.

7

JULY

DEATH AND LOSS

Adolescents can be deeply affected by death
since it explodes the feelings of supremacy that
accompany adolescence. They require careful
nurturing and support to integrate the experience
into their developing understanding of the world.

JULY IS COLD; THE leaves have fallen from the trees and the atmosphere can be austere and demanding. Although winters in South Africa are not harsh relatively speaking, resilience is the key to surviving the dark early mornings and the earlier setting of the sun.

Death – the only certainty in life and a certainty for which we are ill-prepared at the best of times – seems an inappropriate subject in the context of adolescence, yet it lurks as an ever-present, unwelcome possibility. Is it perhaps the last standing taboo about which no one speaks? For an adolescent we, as adults, need to have a deep respect for the trauma an untimely death brings into their lives. It is equally important that as adults we have some understanding of death as we endeavour to support adolescents through this process.

CASE STUDY 18: DEATH OF A PARENT

Keith is a healthy, vibrant 13 year old. His energy is palpable. If only his enthusiasm could be bottled, stored and prescribed for others and, ironically, used one day for him to recover.

His entry to high school has been positive, energetic and enthusiastic. Keith is the epitome of a healthy adolescent ready to take on the world and all it has to offer. Life with all its potential is engaging. He is sporty. He is popular. He is 'cool'. He is reasonable academically. He is charmingly and newly handsome. He comes from a wealthy home. Ostensibly he has it all.

And then as suddenly as an electricity power failure, it all changes. Dad, with whom Keith has an exceptional relationship, is killed in an accident. He was cool, energetic, sporty and fun. He was wealthy and successful.

It is as if the very traits he had so generously given his son are switched off, buried with him. In spite of occasional therapeutic interventions, Keith shuts down. He does not sustain sessions with the therapist. His smile all but vanishes. The energy is replaced with an ennui and a lethargy hard to unravel. Coming to school is a battle. Sport is unthinkable. Studying and focusing on academics is unbearable. Eating is hardly tolerable. His grades decline. Life is awful. His weight begins to take on a life of its own. One month he billows and the next month he is frail.

So it goes for five years. There are days when the thought of washing himself is unbearable. Facing his friends is nightmarish. They don't understand why he can't 'get over it'. He has become 'uncool'; a burden because he is now 'the guy whose dad died'. He tries to win them back by partying as if there will never be another party. He drinks alcohol to stop the pain and to be cool again. He drinks to forget. He smokes. He cuts himself. He cries. He hates his mother for recovering.

He hates school. He hates home. He resents his siblings.

Writing final examinations is a nightmare – for five years Keith has avoided the prospect and it has now come to invade his life relentlessly. His teachers, almost out of patience, have tried to resolve his lack of concentration. Keith scrapes through his final school examinations and limps on into his muddled adult life. Once so complete, Keith has been felled by the death of his beloved father.

CASE STUDY 19: RESPECTING THE PROCESS OF MOURNING

It is break time and Nompumelelo is sad; deeply, deeply sad. Her aunt has passed away. It had been a terrible dying but she hadn't expected the moment of death to happen while she was at school. Her mother had encouraged her to come to school because she knew that soon she would have to miss a number of days for the mourning. Hard as it would have been she wanted to be there for her aunt, right till the end. Instead she had received the news on her cellphone and it seems so cold and unfair.

Her friends had hugged her and then continued eating noisily through the contents of their lunch boxes.

'She is not just an aunt!' she wants to yell, thinking that the other students do not understand that her aunt's death creates a deep, dark void in her life. 'In my culture aunts are like mothers. My aunt loved me and cared for me. My aunt understood me. She lived with us. The lines aren't so clearly drawn, you know. She was one of the most special people in my life.'

Fortunately her favourite music teacher walks past the group and sees Nompumelelo looking very distressed. The teacher knows

Nompumelelo well and knows that her aunt has just passed away, and draws her aside to console and speak to her. Nompumelelo explains numerous concerns to the teacher, who decides to ask the school head to intervene.

Once in the head's office Nompumelelo lets her tears flow. She speaks about what her aunt meant to her and how there will be significant material differences without her aunt in the home. While her aunt has died of liver complications, Nompumelelo knows that her aunt was also HIV positive. 'What if the others in the class hear that?' she asks fearfully.

After a long discussion, which reveals numerous concerns bothering Nompumelelo, her biggest fear is at last expressed. As part of a cultural cleansing ceremony, she is going to be expected to go to the town where her aunt was born. She will have to bath in a mixture of water and chicken blood and she will have to shave her head completely. She will not only need time away from school, but she will also look different and she is worried that she might even smell strange.

Not only is Nompumelelo having to negotiate the very deep pain of losing someone close to her, but she is having to navigate her way around the rituals of a mourning process new to her and possibly foreign to some of her peers.

Cultural differences around death and mourning are important for schools to understand and to tolerate within reason. A careful discussion with the head put Nompumelelo's mind at ease and she felt that she would be allowed to follow the mourning process appropriately. The issue throws into relief the problems schools face in transforming into places that understand and respect many cultures, and how they encourage their communities to respect and understand each other's spaces at significant times.

CASE STUDY 20: THE DEATH OF A CHILD AND A SIBLING

The evening is balmy and beautiful. Raucous hadedas squawk overhead, reminding us that we are in Africa. The Grade 12 class sits at the front of the school, excited by their final prize-giving ceremony: symbolically the evening draws their school careers to a close.

Serene, beautiful, kind beyond measure and almost angelic, a slight young woman sits amongst her peers at the ceremony. She has already received numerous awards for her academic ability. The evening has settled in and various awards have been made, but the finest awards are kept for last. They are the prizes that are voted for by peers and teachers and which recognise characters of exceptional calibre and deep moral fibre. They are highly valued awards that few receive and which invariably mark those that are going to go on to make their mark in the world by improving the lives of others. Kim, loved by her peers and teachers, rises to walk to the stage to receive the award for the most compassionate and caring person in the school. It is a special award, recognising the rare and excellent qualities that human beings have the potential to display, but rarely do. Kim has displayed them consistently for her five years of high school. She is inherently good, gentle and very special.

Her younger sister – beautiful too – beams with pride, as do her parents, who have supported her throughout her school career. Tall, lithe and lovely, the wisp of a young woman on the threshold of her life receives the award to thunderous applause.

Two weeks later, the telephone in the principal's office rings. It seems to pierce the air more shrilly than usual. Kim's father is on the other end of the line. The words are choked across the line. 'Kim is sick. The doctor says it's very serious. The cough she has been struggling with seems to be cancer. It is very bad,' he catches a sob as he tells the sad news to the incredulous principal.

The insidious cancer has crept into her beautiful body and suddenly raged against this beautiful young life. The battle seems interminable, but in reality it is quick. Three months later, unwillingly, beautiful Kim crosses the bar to the life we hope is kept for those good and exceptional people.

The pain for those close to her is unbearable. There are simply no answers to make sense of the loss. Kim's parents are devastated. Their precious, beautiful daughter who was on the threshold of a new phase of her life has gone from them forever. The pain seems unrelenting. Kim's sister cannot comprehend that her older sibling will not be there to share secrets with anymore. School is simply a reminder of her sister. She hates attending classes where Kim sat; seeing trees Kim loved, looking at teachers that Kim knew, is all unbearable. Soon she becomes defined by the fact that she is 'the girl whose sister died'.

Kim's parents visit the school from time to time, trying to manage their grief and that of their daughter. It seems as if the tears will never stop. It seems as if well-meaning but inane and inappropriate comments will hound them forever.

The family attend bereavement counselling and cry with Compassionate Friends. Indeed their lives without their beloved Kimmy will never be the same. Kim's sister feels she will never be able to write exams or finish school. Every piece of work she is required to submit becomes a reminder of what she has lost. For two years she battles through the anguish of having to complete school, but she triumphs in the end because of the support and love of her parents. They have lost one daughter and pour their love into the remaining child. They choose to live for her, acknowledging that it is a new path they are walking. A different set of road signs will have to guide them.

Sometimes the pain overwhelms them and they have to step aside from the grind of life. They feel and acknowledge Kim everywhere but move on slowly. There are new seasons, new joys and while Kim will not be with them physically and the pain remains ever present, they choose life. After counselling and crying and trying new ways to define herself, Kim's sister pulls through on most days. She chooses life above death.

The journey is not easy. Men and women, mothers and fathers all deal with death differently. There are occasionally cavernous potholes along the way, but Kim's family perseveres in the adversity. They choose to remember their serene, beautiful, kind Kim in a way that does not compromise other members of the family. They are brave; they soldier on as torchbearers to others.

Life will never be the same but it continues and Kim whispers to them in the wind and they can be strong.

DEVELOPMENTAL CONSIDERATIONS AND SUGGESTIONS

Everybody deals with death in their own way. It is a very difficult time, whether you are an adult, adolescent or child. Adolescents find death particularly difficult because it is a time when they believe in immortality; especially their own. Dealing with death denies the adolescent the fantasy around immortality.

The experience of death differs according to the depth of meaning that exists within the relationship between the mourner and the deceased. For the adolescent, whether the person is a family member or not is irrelevant since the adolescent reacts to death profoundly. Death compromises the adolescent's sense of safety within the world. Complex emotions and questions arise as a result of death. Psychologically death is not part of adolescence, which is a time of libido and intense living. When adolescents have to confront death it is both intrusive and cruel.

The manner of the death is also significant in how death is felt and managed. Experiences are very different if a loved one dies suddenly in an accident or after illness. If someone important within the relationship commits suicide the understanding of death, the reaction to it and by implication the recovery will be experienced very differently to that of a death that is expected or is the result of an accident. Being with a person at the deathbed is a fantasy of the living because it suggests a time of coming to terms with death and being able to deal with possible flaws that exist in the relationship, but being at someone's deathbed does not necessarily alter the pattern or the pain of mourning.

The stages adolescents experience when negotiating the death of a significant person are not dissimilar to those of adults. Stages of shock, numbness, denial, search, anger, guilt, bargaining and despair are part of the healthy process of mourning

In normal mourning, it is usual and indeed appropriate that the mourners closest to the dead person will feel like dying themselves to try to get rid of the pain, because continuing life without that person seems unbearable. If the mourners had a good relationship with the dead person, as Kim's family had with Kim, it is understandably unbearably painful. If the relationship was an intimate and healthy one, mourners will experience a normal and healthy mourning process, albeit exceedingly painful. Mourning takes different forms as the survivors continue with their lives.

For example, Kim's sister will mourn that her sister is not there to be an aunt to her children one day. Normal mourning is about being able to hold on, as Kim's family did, to the goodness of the person, and to take the memory of the person with them into the future. Men, who are generally socialised not to cry, find themselves weeping at unexpected times. They try to cover their hurt and protect their families and yet they need love and protection too.

The differences in mourning between the mother and father may put added strain on their relationship.

Death can put an enormous strain on a marriage but, carefully worked through, it can also bring a couple together in a meaningful way.

Men tend to withdraw into themselves at a time of personal tragedy and emerge once they have come to some understanding of their grief. They may become very silent. Generally, women want to talk through their pain. They may express their anger and their grief vehemently in order to process their profound loss.

Men's grief can be compounded by the sense that they have traditionally been expected to protect their families and show little vulnerability. Death challenges these stereotypes and a man may have additional burdens to overcome at an already fraught time. Women may accept counselling more readily than men, but once men acknowledge their need they often express enormous relief at having a space where they too can receive support, which in turn enables them to continue to play a supportive role.

For both genders, death devastates the internal world of the person left behind and it is a daunting task for them to slowly rebuild their lives. Reworking this new internal world with the old can be very painful.

In complicated or unresolved mourning one will notice, as is the case with Keith, that the bereaved person does not recover effectively and significant psychotherapeutic intervention, above intense bereavement counselling, is needed. Complicated or extreme mourning presumes that the struggle to get over the death of the person is going to take a very long time, well over the two years that is generally indicated. Keith could not get over the experience of feeling abandoned and of feeling lost in the now different and new relationship with his mother. Family therapy may have assisted Keith because he could have dealt with his problems directly with his mother.

When his father was alive, Keith mirrored him in order that he would love him; with his death, Keith was faced with having to be himself, entirely separated from his father. If he had resolved this overidentification with his father while he was still alive, he may have had a stronger and more separate identification when dealing with his death. When his father died, Keith had nothing to which to adhere or understand himself by. There was no substance left to Keith because the metaphorical mirror through which he understood himself was 'broken'.

Although Keith presented as 'healthy' before the death of his father, there were clearly serious underlying difficulties in the relationship. The death of his father impacted directly on Keith's identity and the difficulties of enmeshed identities were thus more difficult to resolve.

When a person close to them dies, adolescents – like adults – may feel as though a part of them has died. In order to mitigate this particular loss, it is beneficial to help the adolescent bring that part of the self back by asking them to speak about what it was, in particular, that made them so connected to the person. Keith lost the vibrancy that he emulated when his father was alive and he needed to understand that his joyous self belonged to both him and his father and that it would be acceptable to reintegrate that aspect of himself into his identity as his own.

Owing to their tumultuous developmental stage, adolescents do not think about death as consciously as adults do. As discussed in the Introduction, adolescents feel supreme. Given this aspect of adolescence, death can be experienced as far more traumatic and shocking. It can shake their sense of security because death is something their parents cannot fix or resolve.

The death of a meaningful person can bring startlingly significant change to the everyday norm to which the bereaved person is accustomed. Whether it is the death of a sibling, which may cause the remaining sibling to be an only child, or whether the dynamic in a relationship shifts, or whether the death results in an adolescent not having a mother or a father, the shift can be both materially and emotionally difficult to manage. The emotional change arises as the adolescent has to cope with the trauma of losing someone and then continuing life without them.

Adolescents often respond with anger and shock if a friend or loved one commits suicide. Reasons for suicide are complex and sometimes obscure, which makes the death all the more difficult to comprehend. Often teenage suicide arises from the adolescent fantasy that death is a punishment for those remaining behind. Teenagers often fantasise about people mourning for them, but they forget that they will not be there to experience the attention. Parasuicide amongst adolescents occurs when they want to express and communicate feelings of despondency, hopelessness and anger rather than an actual intent to kill themselves. The mourning in the case of suicide is complex for all those affected by it but the abiding emotion felt by adolescents when they lose a friend to suicide is anger.

When someone close or special to them dies, adolescents are often faced with spiritual thoughts and will contemplate more significantly what they believe about life after death, while older adolescents may consider existential notions around the meaning of life. These are important considerations, which require parents and significant adults to be present and attentive.

Attending the person's funeral can be very valuable in recognising the finality of the death of the person. The presence of significant others who are available to offer support for the grieving person may provide the safety required by the bereaved at this vulnerable time. Friends of the bereaved adolescent need to be taught that it is not necessary to have the right words to say but rather that their very presence is meaningful for the recovery of the grieving friend. Friends are vital for the bereaved adolescent and parents will be required to stand alongside their adolescents as they support the friend in crisis.

In our diverse South African society it is important for people, schools and parents to be aware of different cultural practices and rituals. European culture is not the dominant culture and African funeral customs are significant and noteworthy. Rituals in all communities, as mentioned in Case Study 19, are important in the process of mourning since they form a meaningful part of the healing process after bereavement.

While a parent can never fully prepare their adolescent or themselves for death because one cannot grieve a loss until a person has died, one can try to minimise the trauma of the death and dying by helping the adolescent to understand the significance of that person in their life and thus help them integrate these concepts into their own identities.

We would all do well to try to have good, healthy relationships within our families so that in the case of untimely death we can celebrate and integrate all that was good and noble about a loved one. Wise advice it is in Proverbs that tells us 'Never let the sun go down on your anger', and yet we all know how difficult that is to practise in our daily lives.

SUMMING UP

- Although most people experience the loss of loved ones as traumatic, adolescents experience death particularly deeply since it explodes their sense of immortality and supremacy.

- It can take at least two years for the healthy mourning process to take its course and for the grieving person to begin to manage the altered world in which they find themselves.

- Grieving adolescents require patience and support as they experience the process of mourning.

- The topic of death and dying should not be avoided and parents can help their adolescents move towards maturity by guiding them in supporting bereaved friends.

- Hard as it is, we should try to be in good standing with our family members and the special friends in our lives. That does not mean never arguing and always approving; it means always authentically loving those close to us wherever they are at in their development as a human being.

- The loss of a child is one of the worst pains imaginable. The parent's world alters forever and they have to be extremely courageous if there are remaining siblings since those children will need their parents to continue in loving support of them.

- Usually men and women mourn differently, but the pain for both parents is equally intense.

8

AUGUST

TECHNOLOGICAL COMMUNICATION AND THE DIGITAL DIVIDE

Society does not yet fully appreciate the implications of social networking technology for young people, so we need to continue thinking about its meaning, its use and how to work with it. Parenting adolescents in this wonderful and exciting technological age requires parents, as with any aspect of adolescence, to set appropriate boundaries to support the family ethos. This chapter is lengthy since this is complex terrain that requires careful thought and a proactive approach.

AUGUST IS BLUSTERY. OLD leaves that still have a tenuous grasp on trees are given a final shake and the wind sweeps out the dust of winter to make way for the imminent newness of spring. Although August signifies the end of winter, it can be a difficult month, forcing us to draw on resources that may be a little jaded. Dealing with the world of the information superhighway may make parents feel like the last old leaf on the tree, futilely clinging to familiar old branches. Alternatively, some parents will be inspired by the challenge, bluster, awe and excitement brought about by social networking technologies. Regardless of how August makes you feel as a parent, the inexorable challenge of technology, albeit exciting, is new and radically different from the challenges your own parents had to face.

CASE STUDY 21: USING SOCIAL NETWORKING NEGATIVELY

Tony is an attractive, popular, sporty Grade 10 boy who has good face-to-face communication skills, which he has enjoyed since his early childhood. Not only is he naturally a good, confident communicator, but he also has parents who are firm with him about good social manners. He always greets people with respectful direct eye contact and engages peers and adults with gregarious ease.

Tony finds himself in the headmaster's office one morning because he has created a Grade 8 boy's profile on Facebook. The boy, Mark, did not have an existing profile and Tony has created his pseudo-profile at school using the school computers. Mark is a young and unassuming boy. The purpose of the fake profile is for Tony to send rude and crude messages to people that Mark knows.

Mark discovers he has a fake profile on the social networking site when his adolescent friends approach him, angrily demanding to know why he has been so rude. On other occasions girls confront him, saying that they do not want to date him and please not to ask them those sorts of questions on the networking site. Poor Mark is utterly confused and approaches a teacher for help. The teacher quickly realises what has happened and manages to work out who has created the false profile in Mark's name. The teacher takes the issue to the headmaster.

Mark is fortunate in that his friends, once they realise that he has not sent the messages, hold nothing against him. Mark's parents are contacted by the school and they allow the school to deal with the problem, saying they will support Mark if they notice any residual reaction to the unfair and unpleasant treatment he has received. Fortunately for the school, they are interested only in the welfare of their son and do not want to prolong Mark's suffering as a result of Tony's vindictive actions. The parents feel that Tony is the school's problem and the school must deal with him; they want to concentrate on keeping their son whole.

While keeping the legal issue in mind, the headmaster tries to understand what possessed Tony to be so cruelly disrespectful and thoughtless in disregarding the younger adolescent's personal space and identity. The headmaster is aware that Tony appears socially very well adjusted and cannot understand either the need for or the purpose of Tony's behaviour.

Tony explains that through social networking sites such as Mxit and Facebook, he has found it easy to live out his fantasies. He did not think about the consequences of creating the pseudo-profile. The technology is paradoxical. Although it has a distancing effect when working with it, it is immediate in its transmission, yet the emotional reaction at the receiving end is removed from and unknown to the sender. Tony explains that this disjointed sense of time has made it hard for him to feel responsible for his actions.

After Tony has apologised to Mark and his family, the school decides that they will suspend him from his rugby team for the remainder of the season. Tony's family support the school's decision and are grateful because as a family they were also going to punish Tony by not letting him go to gym, owing to his thoughtless actions.

Tony tells the headmaster he found it had become almost too easy to abuse Mark through social networking communication. For example, he says it is easy to imagine you are a powerful individual who has a quick, clever, witty mind, added to which is an incredibly attractive physique, since no one can see your face and whether or not you are in fact the adorable, attractive, 'six-pack' muscle hunk that you project. Behind the screen, in reality, the adolescent may be a pimply-faced, insecure, boring, skinny 16 year old. Although Tony is a reasonably built, confident adolescent, he needs to feel in control. Behind the screen, Tony felt like a god as he created a person whom he could direct to do things. The headmaster discovers that Tony has been feeling insecure and the need to be supreme had overwhelmed him.

Tony confides in the headmaster that he usually feels quite

confident within himself but he had had a fight with his girlfriend prior to the incident, which made him take his anger out through the social network. Tony's reasons are different from those examined in Case Study 22, where a young girl uses the social network because she really does feel inadequate with herself.

CASE STUDY 22: BEING A DIFFERENT PERSONA ON MXIT

From the time Sarah was a little girl, her parents have described her as being shy. She would not easily play with other children in nursery school and kept to herself. Sarah's father acknowledges that he too was like this when young and that he also battled to have friends because he was often incredibly nervous. Her parents describe Sarah as being inappropriate and immature in her communication, which often leads to misunderstandings.

Over the years Sarah has gained a little in confidence but still struggles tremendously in expressing her emotions clearly and confidently to people. She bottles up any perceived negative emotions because she says her family home is very quiet and conflict-free. Sarah feels bad bringing in her hateful or depressed emotions into such a good space. When she tries to show her miserable side, she feels like the mad member in the family, which in turn leaves her hating herself.

In Grade 9, Sarah is called into the headmistress's office because there has been tremendous concern that she has been telling people over Mxit that she is going to kill herself. Her friends also say that she uses Mxit excessively and rarely chats directly to peers. One friend comments that Sarah struggles to make eye contact and her body posture looks odd, as she hunches her shoulders when around others as though she is trying to be invisible.

A disturbing factor is the content in Sarah's communications. She talks about how many 'guys' she wants to 'get with', giving descriptions of when she was with a few guys sexually at the same time. This shocks her parents considerably, as they have considered Sarah an appropriate model for her peers in terms of compliant and quiet behaviour. Her peers also complain that it appears to be Sarah who is posting sexually crude and hurtful messages about others in an 'honesty box' (previous feature of Facebook).

Sarah confesses that she feels very depressed, as she feels like a social freak and struggles to communicate with people face to face. She feels that people misunderstand her and judge her. Saying what she wants to say over social networking helps her because she feels less embarrassed about herself as a result of the sense of distance created by the technology, while at the same time feeling supported by her friends who communicate with her through social networking. Sarah says she knows that her suicidal comments are overwhelming for her friends, but she desperately needs people to hear that she is not coping and that she feels isolated.

She admits that the inappropriately explicit sexual text messages are to make her seem experienced and 'cool'. Sarah confesses that she longs for a boyfriend with whom she can be romantic. Mxit makes it so easy for her to feel normal in communicating with people because through it she experiences positive friendship via text messaging, as though her peers were treating her as they treated their other friends. In public her friends ignore her and make her feel as if her gestures and advances for friendship are irrelevant and inappropriate. When she texts messages she can reinvent herself as someone far removed from the insecure, awkward Grade 9 she hates being in real life.

Through discussion with her parents and the headmistress, Sarah requests psychotherapy; she knows that her way of communicating and what lies beneath it is not good for her well-being. She is eager to improve her personal and social self.

DEVELOPMENTAL CONSIDERATIONS AND SUGGESTIONS

Adolescents in modern society need to cope with constant communication through the mass media and the information superhighway. Internationally, from the late twentieth century adolescents have been versed in and are relaxed with the emerging use of social networking communication. We are dealing with a completely new generation of adolescents: the technology generation. Not only do parents feel the generational divide, but they will also feel the digital divide, particularly if they shy away from keeping up to date with new technologies. Parents have an obligation to be aware of the new communication strategies; however, this does not mean that parents need to attach the same meaning to technology in their lives as adolescents do. Adolescents often complain that they feel uncomfortable when parents act like teenagers on their Facebook profiles or if they communicate with their peers via Facebook.

Another example of new technology for which we do not have the rules and of which we do not know the consequences for adolescents, is the three-dimensional virtual world. In this virtual world a persona is created and travels around the virtual world as an 'avatar'. The avatar represents the individual, who has created the persona with a different name and a virtual physique of their choice. The avatar can travel through a vast range of virtual spaces – natural environments, shopping malls, museums, clubs, homes, apartments and cities. As the new technology gains in popularity, parents and adults will have to consider the impact on adolescents of 'living in' and 'playing in' a virtual world. Presently it seems to be more of an adult playground, with advertisers and companies buying 'real estate' and setting up their virtual corporate offices in this virtual world.

Adults may face a dilemma about managing the new communication successfully since the technology arrived before the etiquette and the rules for using such technology. Most adults have an understanding of telephone etiquette, but few have a sense of internet etiquette. Furthermore, adults are not able to recall their own adolescent use of technology since technology has advanced so much and is still advancing rapidly.

Parents need to give adolescents privacy and adolescents need to learn to take responsibility for their actions both on and off the internet superhighway. The dilemma lies in the fact that parents know that adolescents are not always capable of taking responsibility for their actions, including their actions on the internet or on public social networking sites such as Facebook or Mxit.

While we do not have the answers, we do have some thoughts and suggestions on how to support adolescents in their use of technology. Parents reading this will remember that when they were adolescents, their parents did not know what they were up to for a good deal of the time. Adolescents need space in order to practise being adult. Parents therefore need to give their adolescents privacy in all their communication. Just as parents should not read adolescent's journals, so too parents should never read their technological communication – their Facebook, Mxit, email and text message communication – unless there has been a significant breach of trust which requires intervention.

Adolescents must be made to understand that although Facebook and other social networking sites *appear* to be private, they are in fact very public domains. Because adolescents are typically impulsive and have a sense of immortality, they find it hard to accept the paradox of the simultaneously private and public space inherent in social networking. Adolescents must be prepared to say publicly whatever it is they write on Facebook.

Trust between parents and adolescents should be well established and by now they should have already integrated the parents' value system. It is appropriate for parents to be there to deal with the fallout when the adolescent fumbles with the communication. For example, if an adolescent girl has been inappropriately provocative and seductive in her technological social networking and as a result her reputation has been compromised, be there to support her in re-establishing a more suitable identity.

Just as a parent can experience pain when seeing a toddler fall because they are trying to run faster than they can, so too it is painful to see adolescents injure themselves emotionally or socially when they are acting out destructively rather than thinking through their actions clearly and carefully (the concepts of 'acting out' and 'thinking through' are discussed in Chapter 5). Be alongside the adolescent to think through the mistakes in communication and how the damage done can be repaired. Obviously if the action is repeated, there is a problem that needs to be addressed with more serious intervention since the adolescent is acting out dangerously. If parents insist on being intrusive and if they invade the privacy of adolescent communication, they should expect the adolescent to become more deviant in hiding communication.

It can be very hard for parents not to know what is happening in the social and the internal life of their adolescent. It is, however, appropriate that parents do not know everything, because the adolescent needs to start separating from the parent in order to experience their burgeoning adult world. When parents afford their adolescents appropriate trust, they increase the adolescent's ability to take responsibility for themselves.

A healthy adolescent is technologically savvy, but it is also important that in spite of the digital divide that sometimes exists between parent and adolescent, the parents' needs and personas are also valued. We have found that if parents keep three areas in mind when faced with thinking about and dealing with the use of social networking communication by their adolescents, they will have a good chance of supporting healthy communication in the adolescent and in the home.

The first area to hold in mind is how you usually communicate as a family. The second is to think about how your adolescent's needs are met through the characteristics of social networking. The third is to think about the characteristics of networking communication and the societal context in which they operate. By fitting these areas together effectively, the meaning of your adolescent's communication becomes clear enough so that parents can decide on the necessary support for their adolescent.

Parents can ask themselves if they think they successfully passed the family's values to their adolescent during the toddler age and again in the latency age (about six to nine years). In the process of instilling these values or beliefs, the parents should have used consequences and boundaries to guide their children along the paths they felt were appropriate in order to keep the family's value structure and ethos in place.

Parents always represent necessary adult authority. Remember adolescents have an adult part but also a child part of themselves. Just as they cannot run a family, so they cannot run their communication completely independently.

Firmly entrenched family values go a long way in assisting with managing and effectively assimilating the demands that social networking has placed upon parents. When an adolescent uses mobile phone technologies in your home or car, make rules that support your family values. If, for example, your family values respect the safety and the privacy of others, a parent should not sms while driving or take an excessive number of phone calls when others are in the car and can hear conversations. Just as it is inappropriate to sms or receive phone calls at the dinner table, so it is inappropriate to break communication opportunities through the overuse of cellphones in the car. Often chats in the car can be very special times of connectedness between parents and their children, so the intrusion of mobile phones, MP3 players and other technology should be kept to a minimum.

Hard as it is, try to remain the adult in the face of adolescent development. Survive and understand the rudeness and the hateful emotions that adolescents may express, since they will typically reject the parents' boundaries and desire to move into the perceived safety of their world of secrecy. Try to keep attuned to their development. It is difficult for parents to set boundaries when they are met by hostility but it is worth persevering. Keep in mind that the reason for having rules when parenting adolescents is to help them take on responsibility and live and play ethically in society once they are adults.

When considering what freedom to give your adolescent in social networking ask: What responsibility is your adolescent capable of? For example, in a group setting does your adolescent show good manners by letting everyone have their say? This type of behaviour would be indicative of an adolescent attuned to appropriate communication etiquette, which is likely to be followed through during social networking communication. If at any stage you observe that your adolescent on Mxit is not following through on the good manners you expect, for example, then discipline the adolescent as if they were rude in public.

A parent may decide to deprive an adolescent of time in front of television – or whatever is appropriate for that particular family setting – if technology is abused. In Case Study 21, if Tony's parents thought his communication to a fellow family member was extremely disrespectful they may have had a rule in the home that they believed befitted the misdemeanour. For example, his communication was disrespectful, therefore taking away a mode of communication, such as his computer, would be an appropriate and logical punishment as he has not shown responsibility in this area. We disagree with the punishment given by the school by not allowing Tony to play rugby, because this punishment does not logically link with his destructive communication behaviour. We encourage natural logical consequences to poor behaviour; the severity of the punishment must fit the behaviour. The same rule would apply for any networking communication. When parents are satisfied that their adolescent has learned from their poor behaviour, more gratifying rewards should be granted.

Growing up is a gradual process. As your adolescent shows more responsibility, so you may slowly withdraw your consequences to their misdemeanour. This will allow them to be more responsive to taking on adult behaviour. It is about knowing how much responsibility they are able to manage effectively. If they let you down, step in and reset previous reasonable boundaries until they show a healthy independence and an ability to manage the given technology appropriately.

For example, if they cannot let go of the mobile phone until midnight and are depriving themselves of good sleep and relevant study time, then parents will need to step in and help them feel safe and in control of their communication behaviour. It will be necessary to set time frames around the use of the mobile phone until poor habits are broken. One rule could be that at a certain time in the evening, adolescents put their phones on the kitchen table and parents should not expect to have to follow up that they have done so.

Banning your adolescent from the world of technology is effectively inhibiting their effective progress into the world that exists beyond school. In addition it is not the technology that is problematic, but rather the fact that it is used *inappropriately*.

Parents may find it helpful to ask themselves in what way they may be breaking their normal parenting ethos to manage their adolescent's use of social networking communication. Parenting social networking should be similar to parenting the adolescent's primary face-to-face family communication.

At what point does the use of the mobile phone occur in your adolescent's life? For example, do you as a parent see your adolescent using the mobile phone during the initial stages of a new relationship, which would indicate shyness, or is the mobile phone used throughout a relationship, which would indicate immaturity? Does social networking communication represent your adolescent's struggle to engage directly or does it reflect unhappiness with the identity they present to the world in day-to-day communication? The answers you, as a parent, give to these questions will help you understand how the technology is being used by your adolescent and whether it is appropriate or not. If the answers you give suggest that the adolescent has an underlying dissatisfaction with their identity, then additional help will be required to assist them to integrate their personality and sense of self more effectively.

In Case Study 22 Sarah had poor communication skills and an insecure sense of self, so she used Mxit as a defence against her vulnerabilities. The usefulness of the technology meant that she was able to make some connection in order to gain help.

In Case Study 21 Tony was not a poor, shy communicator; quite the opposite. His behaviour can remind parents of the immaturity in adolescents and their need for parental wisdom to help them become more thoughtful and grown up and how to deal with the more angry and retaliatory part of themselves. In the case of Tony, it is important to realise that even though he presented as a controlled, happy adolescent, his actions indicated underlying anxieties that needed to be addressed.

Parents could ask themselves whether their adolescent shows a preference for Mxit or social networking because they find it a safer and more accessible form of communication in a relationship than face-to-face communication. Does social networking communication represent healthy or unhealthy communication? Does social networking communication occur specifically in breaks between direct contact with friends, or during holiday breaks, or rather whenever your adolescent impulsively needs to communicate with a friend? How satisfied are you that social networking communication is helping your adolescent to grow up in a balanced way and to move towards being a mature young adult?

These questions are guidelines to help parents think about their adolescent's relationship with technological communication. In responding to the answers to these questions, parents need to be mindful that it is a time of letting go and allowing the adolescent to solidify their own identity. It is, however, necessary for parents to set boundaries and limits and excessive use of technology that detracts from academic time and important face-to-face communication is unhealthy. We recommend that a time limit for screen time be set.

(Screen time includes television, computer and mobile phone time.) Screen time can be increased during holiday periods but should be monitored carefully during the school term as adolescents can forget that social networking can take up hours of valuable learning time.

Schools, like families, will have a specific communication ethos and the adolescent's communication will need to be respectful of that ethos. Obviously, if parents think the school significantly misunderstands their adolescent, they should step in. Remember that the experience and consequence of this could be tantamount to a family interfering with another family's way of bringing up the children. (Considerations about approaching the school are made in Chapter 11.)

Sometimes, both the family and the school need to reflect on whether their restrictions – or lack of restrictions – support a healthy ethos. Engage with the school if your ethos is different from the school's, and likewise be aware if your unhealthy family behaviour colludes with the school's choosing to ignore or underplay unhealthy behaviour in your adolescent. In tense moments it can be normal not to think clearly about how to respond to situations. In hindsight, the school and Tony's parents could have reflected that Tony probably learned very little about his freedom of communication from not playing rugby or going to gym. He would have been far more affected by a punishment that related to his use of social networking, such as taking away his computer, as this would remind him of the pain he caused and his need to work on the aggressive, destructive side of his personality.

When we consider how an adolescent uses technology, it is important to take developmental considerations into account. In their move from dependence to independence, adolescents feel anxious, vulnerable and impulsive because they are moving away from safe, known relationships and into uncertain and different relationship terrain. Adolescents protect themselves from the dependent state by developing independent defences, such as pseudo-maturity and acting out (explained in Chapter 5). There is an important conflict between a wish for autonomy and a regressive pull to dependence. Obviously, these generalisations about adolescent feelings and experiences should be challenged and parents need to allow the adolescent's true and unique voice or difficult emotions to emerge.

Adolescents will defend themselves in the move towards more mature conversation by pushing boundaries or engaging in communication that has fewer boundaries, such as cyber-communication via text messaging, emails, Mxit and other social networking sites. A communication that eliminates the boundary of time and a physical boundary, and where they can be intrusive at their choice, is extremely desirable to adolescents. For example, adolescents love to be able to send an impulsive thought through Mxit at midnight if they so wish. No thought is given to the fact that they may be intruding on a friend's sleep.

There are heightened aggressive and sexual emotions and drives within adolescents. We need to remember that developmentally it is a physical time for adolescents and that this is likely to be manifested one way or another in their behaviour. The adolescent is still learning to experience what can be felt as an assertive interaction and what can come across as aggressive and inappropriate. Tony was not mindful enough of his serious aggressive communication and learned his lesson unfortunately through hurting someone.

One can see in both Case Study 21 and Case Study 22 that social networking is a powerful form of communication that can offer a channel for vague and unexpressed emotions and fantasies around sexual attraction and aggressive abuse. This is where social networking communication is problematic, since it is often impossible and inappropriate to keep track of adolescent activity on the internet. If the adolescent is out of control or destructive in the way they communicate, we need to reset old boundaries and treat them according to their behaviour. If they are not mature enough to separate what they want to do from what they should do, they need boundaries to be set by their parents.

There are choices and consequences. Consistently monitor the adolescent's behaviour until they no longer act out and instead take ownership of their feelings. A helpful thought may be to ask: To what extent does my adolescent own his destructive and sexual urges and in what way is he channelling them in cyberspace communication? Again, if the parents are not satisfied that appropriate responsibility is present in their adolescent, consequences that fit the family ethos need to be implemented.

The more violence we are exposed to, the more brutalised we are likely to become. We need to remember that we have a choice and that there are fitting consequences to those choices, and it is valuable to make adolescents aware of the choices and the concomitant consequences. Having said this, we do not think computer games, in moderation, and which do not compromise academic learning time, are out of place unless the adolescent starts to 'act out' inappropriately.

Reality can be very hard for adolescents. They have to learn to accept the body they have, their developing personality, the parents they have and reality in general. Generally adolescents will avoid reality and try to live in a fantasy world that has no room for disillusionment, negative feelings or the need to take ownership of difficult emotions. Sometimes adolescents aim to eliminate reality entirely. They will use objects to satisfy the need to deal with reality. One of the most popular of these objects is the mobile phone, which figuratively holds a space for adolescents to communicate their unexpressed fantasies, especially aggressive and sexual ones.

Adolescents perceive the time gap between face-to-face chats with friends as longer than adults do and they may want a type of communication that gives a sense of their being held in mind. Because they tend to experience the 168 hours in a week to be far longer than adults do, adolescents will seek a form of communication that reflects their sense of urgency. Adolescents sometimes cannot cope with containing their need to express emotions immediately. Hence we see the instant gratification through mobile phone technology and social networking sites on the internet.

Adolescents are still developing into their adult selves and thus we can experience them as quite confusing and capricious when observing them with their mobile phones. For example, they can sometimes seem to enjoy being a compassionate listener and at other times a very impatient, unsympathetic and demanding friend. It is our role to help them integrate all the different parts of themselves.

For example, Sarah in Case Study 22 felt like a 'cool player' sending overt sexual messages to friends in their honesty boxes, not thinking once about why she was doing this. While it is their choice – as it was Sarah's – to choose an action, adolescents need to be reminded of the consequences of their actions and to remember that the after-effects of consequences last longer than the action they have taken. Through psychotherapy, Sarah realised that it gave her an emotional rush to send people perverted messages as she imagined them feeling helpless, confused and inadequate sexually. This is how she felt on a daily basis and she wanted others to feel similarly. She struggled for a good year before friendships could be re-established because her peers did not trust her.

Adolescents are often prone to acting out, as discussed in Chapter 5. Acting out is behaviour that represents the feeling or thought of the individual that has not been properly worked through. The action therefore 'holds' the unwanted feeling or thought. There is a dissonance between their actions and their personas. For example, Sarah was acting out on Mxit when she portrayed herself as a very brazen 18-year-old sex goddess, when in reality she was a conservative, quiet and shy adolescent. The meaning of the dissonance however, can be worked through with the parent during face-to-face family interactions. In our experience it appears that acting out behaviour is becoming more understood by parents, as they become increasingly attuned to adolescents' needs and fears.

In Chapters 3 and 4 we encouraged parents to look at the family patterns as they may be played out in adolescents; the same is true of how an adolescent may be communicating through technology. If there is a problem in how your adolescent communicates in cyberspace, look within the home first. Most families hope to encourage non-judgemental communication in the home, usually and hopefully in an environment that displays love and care. One would expect the adolescent to take on what the family ethos has modelled. For example, Sarah's father was aware of his difficulty with communication so he could empathise with Sarah's communication struggles.

Communication in the home is concurrently verbal and non-verbal. Exactly how this dialogue occurs in the family depends on the preference of the family members. Valuable understanding is gathered through verbal communication, where the parent is able to interpret and work through the meaning of the dialogue with their adolescent. Valuable understanding is also gathered through non-verbal cues, such as facial expression, body language and the expression in the eyes. Parents will have experiences of their adolescents showing a look of contempt without uttering a word. Perhaps parents will recognise that they too express intense emotions facially and the adolescent has learned from this. The adolescent is likely to continue similar communication in cyberspace.

Mobile phones are extremely advanced. They usually have internet access, have a facility to communicate with several people simultaneously, can take photographs and have the capacity to download the latest music. Dealing with this communication as a parent is not easy. The media have highlighted the problematic and abusive potential of mobile phones. For example, adolescents have sent photographs of their genitals to friends and strangers, and owing to their immaturity, they have not thought of present or future consequences. Parents cannot practically monitor their adolescents' use of their mobile phones, just as they cannot monitor their daily face-to-face conversations. Therefore it is a matter of instilling self-discipline so that no matter what communication crosses the path of your adolescents, they will respond in a constructive and appropriate way.

Mxit and Facebook can communicate rich emotional material to friends because complex, idiosyncratic, indirect communication is possible. For example, an adolescent may use non-verbal, visual symbols such as smiles (e.g. (:-) or ☺) or CAPITAL LETTERS to highlight the intensity of feelings or thoughts that the adolescent may not comfortably express orally. Social networking communication could be described as a tool that accesses or extends to both the hearing and visual senses. The communication is not as valuable as the intimacy of a direct interaction, yet it is most appealing to an adolescent in terms of the ability to make contact if the adolescent is physically unable to or, more typically, does not desire the awkwardness of direct contact.

The impact of text on the sender and receiver seems to be similar to that of written letters – both are powerful forms of communication and both have the potential of working with the receiving and giving of intense feelings. Similar to letter writing, text messaging enables adolescents to enjoy autonomy as they have control of time, space and pace during the communication. Text messaging can be sent on an emotional high, whereas letter writing has a more formal etiquette and there is an implied delay between sending and receiving, and then replying. Letters do not offer the speed and immediacy that adolescents perceive as so necessary to their ability to communicate. In addition, adolescents experience relationships being equal in social networking, unlike communication in a letter. For example, in Case Study 22 Sarah felt an equal to her peers when communicating via Mxit, whereas in direct communication she explained that she never felt adequate enough to be considered as good as them.

Social networking communication is open to substantial misinterpretation because everybody has their own inner thoughts and experiences. Reading this very sentence, for example, a reader may drift off thinking of when they were misunderstood by a friend, while another reader may be thinking of how they are never misunderstood because they communicate clearly. Knowing exactly what the authors meant would mean meeting them directly and engaging in conversation around the sentence. Parents would be able to pick up the nuances of the tone of the authors' voices and watch their body language.

Adolescents are not interested, not mature enough and do not want to think about implied, subtle nuances – they are too impulsive to check their style and clarity of meaning.

Text messaging offers both the possibility of immediate, direct response as well as the space to think and wait in private. In private, an adolescent can share secrets, daydream and express difficult emotions, which cannot be shared with real people. The diarylike thinking seen on Facebook stands between daydreaming and the objective world, between make-believe and reality. Likewise, text messages can be experienced as in between the objective and subjective realms. This privacy is, however, deceptive as there is a large audience of strangers looking, watching and listening and thus the certainty of privacy is out of the adolescent's control, as much as they feel that this is not so.

Using social networking communication involves ethical issues of confidentiality. The adolescent needs to be aware of possible breaches in confidentiality when using email, text messaging, Mxit and Facebook communication and should keep this in mind when responding. Most adolescents have sole access to their mobile phones but the nature of Mxit and Facebook is about exposure and adolescents are known to share their personal material from mobile phones as well. Their social world tends to blur boundaries and disregard privacy as practised in the adult world.

Adolescents need to presume a continuation of their identity in social networking communication. For example:

- Is there is an established relationship with the person with whom the adolescent is communicating?
- Is all communication they practise similar? Is the needy, vulnerable and dependent part of the adolescent being expressed in the extreme on Mxit?
- Is the confident, independent, responsible part of the adolescent being abusive or taking advantage of not having to have direct contact with a person that is being avoided

or who is despised? Through being aware of inappropriate or avoidance behaviour, adolescents can use social networking communication either to strengthen a responsible voice or entrench vulnerable, avoidant and weak emotional patterns.

- Can adolescents rely on friends to respond in social networking communication in the way that they do in face-to-face communication? It may be worth examining this question with your adolescent.
- Adolescents should be encouraged and challenged to hold all parts of their identities in mind and then question whether they are taking the fantasy too far in their technological communication. Many thinking adolescents understand the inadequacies inherent in using social networking technology as their main source of communication. They feel sorry for their peers who are unable to connect meaningfully outside of social networking arenas.
- 'Rapid change' is the description given to the social climate of the twenty-first century, which has been marked by major and rapid strides in internet and cellular phone technology. The challenging repercussions of these changes in society as a whole and families in particular demand a well-considered and proactive response in terms of parenting.

SUMMING UP

- It is appropriate that parents should **not** know what their adolescents are doing and thinking all the time, yet they are then faced with a dilemma: they need to give adolescents privacy, yet are aware that they will not be fully adult and responsible in their technological communication. It is about dealing with the fallout and supporting them in moving forward if mistakes are made.

- The use of mobile phones is part of a whole communication process for an adolescent's expression of developmental needs and emotions. It should never compete for primary position with face-to-face communication.

- The meaning of your adolescents' use of the communication determines whether you quietly support their move to adulthood or whether you step in to help them deal with destructive consequences of their behaviour.

- The parent will assist the development of the adolescent if they uphold principles and ground rules when parenting. Think of and possibly verbalise the adolescent's developmental needs in front of them and so learn about how their needs are met through the characteristics of the social networking communication.

- Reflection on the issues discussed can lead to an adolescent who is able to communicate and integrate interactions both on a face-to-face and on a social networking level.

9

SEPTEMBER

PHYSICAL BODY ISSUES

In this chapter the case studies look at adolescents'
relationships with their bodies and how they try
to hide or alter them in order to feel better about
themselves.

LIGHTNESS SHOULD BE IN the air. The new greenness budding on the trees is at odds with the chilly breezes and cruel drops in temperature. Spring flowers and fragrances abound and life should seem so alive with possibility. In reality though, beautiful as it may be, September's beauty belies that it is the month of extremes. Spring is so much like an adolescent about to embark on their wonderful young adult journey: promise and hope abound and yet so often panic and dissatisfaction lie just beneath the surface.

CASE STUDY 23: THE OBSESSION WITH THE IDEAL BODY

Cape Town weather is acting up on this particular September day: it is grey and miserable, much the way Cara feels some days. There is no sense of the joy of spring or the hope that attends some adolescents. Cara has disinvested from the process of school and clings to the thought of the day she can leave school and make her own decisions. She feels she has had enough of other people telling her what to do and when to do it. School is an all-too-ordinary space for her since she slumped into the easy mantle of mediocrity at the beginning of her high school career. Her parents separated years before her school career started and her mother has recently married her partner. Cara likes her stepfather, especially because he doesn't nag and he encourages her to take school easy. Cara finds her mother, on the other hand, to be stressed and too ambitious for her daughter.

Throughout high school Cara has struggled with her body image. 'If only I had bigger breasts or smaller thighs,' she often moans to her mother. She spends hours obsessively examining minor flaws and contemplating what would make her happier. Her body shape is blamed for her not having friends, for her poor academic performance, for her general malaise; yet Cara's body is typical of her age and her gender.

On one particularly wet and miserable day she approaches her mother and asks if she can suggest a birthday present for her seventeenth birthday. Hoping that Cara will not ask for a car, her mother bravely agrees. Cara drops the bombshell: 'I want my C-cup made bigger and I want liposuction on my thighs. I have spoken to a plastic surgeon who has told me what it will cost and he can do it next holiday before exams and stressful stuff.'

When Cara's mother regains her ability to speak, she begins a tirade of reasons for Cara not to have the surgery. Cara is adamant and so begins an insistent demand for the surgery. Cara's mother just as adamantly refuses. Relieved to be going on a week-long business trip, Cara's mother sees the time away from her daughter's nagging as a respite. Instead of confronting her daughter's issues, she assumes they will disappear. Adolescents rarely let their issues disappear!

The respite is short-lived. On her return from her business trip, Cara's mother is informed that the operation has been booked and that her husband, Cara's stepfather, has given her the funds for the surgery and signed the relevant consent forms.

By not addressing and acknowledging her daughter's issue, Cara's mother has inadvertently caused Cara to expedite her decision in a typically adolescent and not necessarily appropriate manner.

CASE STUDY 24: CHANGING THE BODY FOR ACCEPTANCE

Sizwe trundles into the classroom. He is new to the school and worse still he has come in the middle of the term. Everyone is settled, sorted and in their place. He is the odd guy out. Not only is he one of the few black boys in this school, he has an accent that shouts 'difference' every time he opens his mouth. He speaks with a beautiful, old BBC-style, perfect English accent. His once-exiled parents have come home – well, to *their* home. This place isn't really home for him. He feels his difference keenly. Worse still, he feels he has nothing much to recommend him to the other boys. An avid reader, Sizwe finds the boys' obsession with rugby not only foreign but also rather banal.

When he speaks, the other boys mock him for pretending to be what he is not. When he runs they tease him because 'blacks are supposed to be fast'; when he changes for the physical education sessions, which he hates, he is laughed at because of his physique – he is small compared to his peers. Books are his solace, but the pain of being in a foreign place where he cannot even converse with people perceived to be his own renders his life nightmarish.

And then Sizwe meets John. It is an unlikely partnership. John is huge. He doesn't like reading but he loves rugby. He is a sensitive and kind person. His mother has encouraged him to befriend Sizwe and has given John a lecture on the history of the country. John is popular and it is easy for him to step out of a group. Soon Sizwe is going to the gym with John and building up his muscle strength. Being friends with John helps him to be accepted, but he soon notices that going to gym also gives him status.

Sizwe's interest in his physique becomes an obsession. He instructs his mother to buy him special protein shakes to help build his muscles. Reading gives way to excessive gyming, but it helps Sizwe feel better about himself. By the year end, Sizwe, while never truly one of the boys, is proud of his body.

And then one weekend in the holidays, in order to prove his manliness once and for all, Sizwe decides to visit a tattoo parlour and have a lizard tattooed on the back of his neck. The edge of the lizard's protruding tongue sneaks indefinably above the collar line of his shirt, but the body of the reptile is well hidden by the shirt. The tattoo, he feels certain, will give him all the status he craves.

Initially Sizwe does not show his mother the tattoo – in front of his friends he is proud of it and yet in front of his mother he is embarrassed. A few weeks later with the lizard on the back of his neck far from his mind, Sizwe walks to his bedroom from the shower with just a towel around his waist. His mother steps into the passage behind him and asks what the 'bruise' is on his neck. When his mother sees that it is in fact a tattoo, her apoplexy turns to anger and then anguish. Where has she lost her little boy?

CASE STUDY 25: HIDING THE BODY FROM PUBLIC VIEW

Lindiwe is lovely. Lithe and athletic, intelligent, hard working and blessed with supportive, successful parents, she should be happy. Instead Lindiwe takes her tall, skinny frame and tries to wrap herself into an insignificant minor representation of who she is. She relishes winter because she does not have to remove her jersey and reveal her arms, which she thinks are too thin. Summer is a nightmare and she hates teachers who insist that she removes her jersey because they are too hot. For Lindiwe it is more bearable to be hot than to reveal to the world her shape, her perceived ugliness and the weakness and frailty her thin arms suggest.

After three years of curling into herself and not participating in events that require her to expose her frame, Lindiwe makes what she recalls afterwards as the most significant step of her high school career. A young teacher has noticed her withdrawal into her body and into her jersey in summer and gently confronts Lindiwe. Instead of telling her to remove her jersey and pull herself together, she resonates with Lindiwe's feelings and encourages her to see what would happen if she removed her jersey just once in class. It will be their secret and the teacher promises that if anyone ridicules Lindiwe's arms, she will sort the problem out. A few weeks after the suggestion, Lindiwe tentatively removes her jersey in the classroom. Only the teacher notices, and smiles. Lindiwe is set free from her own limiting perceptions.

Some will read this and think that Lindiwe was being silly, but they fail then to see the enormous courage it took to take the first step of moving into being the person she could be, and indeed what she went on to become.

CASE STUDY 26: FEAR OF PHYSICAL CHANGE

Lebogang is big for her age, but she is still very young and unsophisticated in her ways. Her large brown, doelike eyes speak of her gentleness and playfulness and also of her fear as she enters the frightening space of high school.

She is dropped off at boarding school on her first day and when her mother drives out of the driveway, big welts of tears melt down her face. For the entire first few months of high school she feels desperately alone, even though her personality endears her to her contemporaries in the boarding house.

Although often tearful, Lebogang begins the process of settling into her new life. Suddenly, almost as if overnight, she withdraws into herself completely. She becomes furtive – almost angry – defensive and silent. No one can understand the change that has come over her. Her new-found friends grow tired of her bristly tone of voice and her silences. The boarding house staff are perplexed.

One morning, suddenly and quite uncharacteristically, Lebogang runs out of the classroom during the middle of a lesson. Aware that there have been some concerns about her aloof behaviour, the teacher follows her to the bathroom, where she finds her sobbing uncontrollably.

A less patient teacher would have given up on her, but the teacher persists and eventually Lebogang confides that she fears she is dying because she is bleeding from 'down there'. Flabbergasted that a twenty-first century adolescent could be unaware of a menstrual cycle, the teacher is taken aback at first but then begins to explain to Lebogang that what she is experiencing is in fact to be celebrated as an entry into womanhood.

The school had assumed that the topic of menstruation had been covered by the junior schools that sent students to the high school. They had not dealt with menstruation outside of the Life Sciences curriculum for years, but now it is clear that they have to make amends to their curriculum. In addition, it becomes important for the school to discuss the different cultural contexts around the onset of menstruation so that traditions could, where appropriate, be honoured.

If parents send their children to boarding school, they must prepare them for imminent changes in their bodies and share the process with them rather than fearing the physical signs along the journey to adulthood. Not speaking about imminent physical changes shrouds the changes in fear and can cause problems with the adolescent's self concept to arise.

CASE STUDY 27: BEAUTY AND THE BEAST

Fatima, in Grade 8, is extremely excited about the first spring dance that is taking place at school that Friday. She dreams all week of how beautiful she is going to look in her latest gear, and she imagines herself being kissed by Mark, her dream guy. But there is one dread Fatima has: her skin. Although she does not have significant skin problems, she does have a few spots and she cannot bear hanging out in a group and being in close contact with boys because she feels that she looks like a spotty beast. 'Never fear,' she consoles herself, 'thank goodness for make-up!'

Fatima's mother is opposed to her practising what she terms 'vain rituals' and she forbids Fatima from covering her skin with make-up. Not having any success in negotiating the make-up issue with her mother and resigned to the fact that her painful embarrassment will never be understood or appreciated by her, Fatima does what she always does to overcome this obstacle: she puts on her make-up at her friend's house. They leave from there for the dance and Fatima thinks her mother will be none the wiser.

Fatima enjoys herself and has a wonderful social experience, even though she does not kiss Mark. She feels confident and beautiful.

All hell breaks loose on Monday morning and Fatima's mother takes Fatima with her to see the school psychologist. Her mother fulminates that Fatima has become a deceitful and untrustworthy individual and insists that the school monitor her behaviour and report back to her.

Ironically it was Fatima who had inadvertently alerted her mother to the make-up saga. Wanting to include her mother in her happiness, Fatima had sent photos of herself via her cellphone to her mother because she thought she looked so pretty and she wanted her mother to see the photos. She had forgotten that she had make-up on.

Fatima used the meeting as an opportunity to express her true despair about being seen as a 'criminal' because she loved make-up. With a third party mediating, her mother heard Fatima clearly for the first time: that it was not that Fatima disliked her face, it was just that she struggled being a teenager with spotty skin and the make-up made her feel more confident. Fatima asked her mother, 'Mum, when you are having a "feel ugly" day, don't you sometimes put on your prettiest jewellery and wear your favourite perfume because it helps you feel lovely?' With the counsellor's guidance they agreed that lying was not acceptable but her mother undertook to try and be attuned to her daughter's needs, thoughts and emotions; in this case, Fatima's dream and enjoyment of feeling and looking pretty was important.

CASE STUDY 28: GROWING UP CAN BE HUMILIATING

Thomas is in Grade 9 and generally he is a flourishing adolescent. Best at nothing but game for everything, Thomas is keen to join the school's debating team. It is a place to make friends with peers he admires because of their sharp intellect.

In spite of being younger than the other boys in the team, Thomas is given a chance to debate in a competition against a well-known girls' school. He is anxious but excited. 'When you are anxious, just prepare harder,' the astute coach advises. Thomas sets to doing some intense research in order to hone his arguments and ideas. He practises hard.

When the evening of the debate arrives, he feels prepared and ready, albeit nervous. Sweaty palms and a slight tremor in his newly broken voice give away his nervous excitement. When it is his turn to speak, he takes to the podium with a remarkable presence and his argument slices through the air, until when making a final significant point in his almost flawless presentation, his voice lets him down. What was to be a scintillating conclusion becomes a high-pitched, squeaky closing point. A beginner on a violin would have been no contest for the jarring chords that emanate from his throat.

The adolescent audience laughs loudly. Visibly hurt, Thomas hunches his shoulders and, utterly humiliated, shuffles back to his seat. The older boy next to him puts his arm around him in an overt sign of support – how valuable that show of caring would prove as Thomas tried to regain his composure. To make matters worse, when his opponent stands up to speak, she attacks not his argument, but the squeaky voice. He feels his mortification will never end and he hates the girl intensely for remarking on a normal physical flaw that is simply a sign of the process of growing up.

It takes encouragement from not only his peers but also the adults to enable Thomas to continue debating. Fortunately they are able to focus on his obvious ability. Thomas is able to understand that his voice breaking is in itself something to be honoured in his move towards manhood.

DEVELOPMENTAL CONSIDERATIONS AND SUGGESTIONS

From the moment of birth our human bodies are inextricably linked to our identities. Babies feel everything, be it pain or joy, through their physical bodies because they have not yet developed emotional understanding. If a toddler is feeling sad, he will understand the anxiety in terms of a physical pain. Parents, during this stage of infancy, respond to the physicality of their child by being tactile in their nurturing. Typical parenting actions would include holding, rocking, rubbing or wrapping the infant up tightly to comfort them. Through the relationship with their own bodies, infants thus develop a physically comfortable state of being.

In adolescence this acceptance of and comfort with the body may change as a result of the significant increased physiological growth. Skeletal and muscular development are more rapid than the learning required to make use of the new muscle mass easily and adroitly. At times, it is difficult for parents to remember that their adolescents are trying to catch up emotionally with their physical growth. Even more significant are the growth patterns of strength and skill, which clearly differentiates adolescence from recent childhood. Generally boys overtake girls in terms of physical strength owing to the accelerated production of male hormones, which increase muscular strength. Given the rapid growth happening at different times, adolescents are often described as clumsy, although adults certainly can admire their youthful vigour, skill and speed; nevertheless the change can be so radical that it is alarming for both parents and adolescents.

It is to be expected that adolescents will suffer from anxieties and worries, partly because they are getting to know their new bodies, and also because their physiques will differ from some of their peers who are considered perfect. Parents, other significant adults and teachers must be thoughtful and keenly sensitive to adolescents' delicate developing relationship with their bodies. Negative or judgmental comments around weight, physique and size should be avoided, since eating disorders are easily triggered at this fragile time. (Eating disorders are complex and arise for numerous reasons, this being only one possible cause.)

Adolescents need to be aware that there will be differences of physique and differences in the timing of physical development between one adolescent and another. Many boys will enter high school looking tiny, young and vulnerable, while their peers of the same age may seem like fully grown men. It is hard work for parents to be understanding of the difficulties these differences can bring. Underdeveloped boys may feel vulnerable and inadequate and will need a great deal of reassurance that they will grow, that they will sprout a beard and their voices will break.

It can be a very cruel time for boys and girls as they compare their bodies and their physical development with their peers. Often boys who mature early are inadvertently rewarded for their physique and are often considered more mature and more able. Teachers have to guard against making judgements around physical appearance and development and parents have to be aware that the physique of a child should not determine their response to that child. Smaller adolescents are often mollycoddled and not allowed to grow up, while bigger adolescents are afforded inappropriate levels of responsibility.

Parents often struggle with the realisation that their adolescent has become a fully fledged sexual being with all the concomitant complications that brings. Fathers may feel threatened and uncomfortable with the strength of their sons and mothers may feel inferior compared to their daughters. Parents need to be mindful of their own feelings at this time and should guard against transposing their own inadequacies and fears onto their adolescents. Parents need to keep their issues around their bodies and their other concerns separate from the needs of their adolescents.

Plastic surgery offers all of us the illusion that we can actualise a persona and we can imagine having the ideal body. Breast augmentation may result in or indicate the strengthening of an erotic, healthy part of the self. If, however, the enlargement is associated with underlying inadequacies or immaturity, the action could be potentially destructive. Theory points out that some surgeons 'fail to grasp the toxic shame that can be unleashed by their promises and skill,' encouraging 'potentially devastating pathologies of appearance' (Kilborne, 2002, p 114).

In Case Study 23, Cara's body has not completely developed and surgery may interfere with natural growth. Secondly, Cara is emotionally immature and she would be susceptible to rejecting her body, since she has barely had time to relate to it. Cara's mother could ask if Cara feels the need to be more of an ideal sex object than an integrated person and she could investigate why Cara feels inadequate about her present sexual body. Cara's mother, knowing her daughter, could try to understand whether Cara's request is consistent with her poor self-image or whether there is a dissonance between her physical and emotional maturity. Since Cara has no physical defects in her body and is not lacking in breast tissue, the desire for plastic surgery certainly points to a more deep-seated need within her psyche.

Theory explains that patients seek plastic surgery in order to correct a real or imagined defect in their physical appearance or in their mental perception of their physical appearance. According to Lorand (1961), there are three groups who typically obtain plastic surgery: those who need an operation and are emotionally well; those who are psychologically troubled who need an operation; and those with a pampered sense of self who do not need an operation. In order for the operation to be optimal, it must not only correct an imperfection, but also needs to significantly improve the psychological perception the person has of themselves. Contra-indication for plastic surgery would involve psychological problems of exhibitionism or hypochondria.

Cara's mother hoped the problem would disappear. Instead of wishful thinking, she would have served Cara better had she acknowledged Cara's sense of inadequacy. Cara was projecting her own perceived inadequacies onto her body shape, rather than addressing the reality that was her body.

Parents would do well to discuss the actual body shape of their adolescent with them. Adolescents need to understand that their bodies, in most instances, are predetermined by genetics. They are tall or short, dark or light, heavy or slightly built on account of genes, and while they can keep their bodies healthy through exercise and proper nutrition, their basic body shape is not entirely in their control. The sooner they can come to terms with their bodies and value them for what they can do for them, the more confident and happy they will be about their physical selves.

Nevertheless, adolescents should be encouraged to exercise regularly and eat healthily, since these are important patterns for parents to set down. Exercising as a family can also be a bonding exercise, but caution must be taken if exercise becomes an area for unhealthy competition about build and physique between the generations within the family unit. In Cara's case, she should have been encouraged to exercise to decrease the size of her thighs rather than resorting to liposuction. The latter solution suggests that Cara relies on instant gratification and is unable to work towards a goal healthily.

Lindiwe, in Case Study 25, tries to hide her body in her jersey. Strange as it may seem, it is evident that Lindiwe is appropriately struggling through developing a comfortable relationship with all the parts of her body. Having an adult who is kind, patient and mindful of the exaggerated fear that Lindiwe feels, assists her to start being able to relate to her body in a non-threatening and safe manner. Lindiwe learns to come to accept her changing body and recognise that avoiding the reality of her body is disadvantaging her ability to be spontaneous. Lindiwe explained how she perceived her skin as feminine and sexy, a part of her new persona that she hated. She wanted to remain being a child. Her arms were linked to her developing breasts, which she also perceived as a reminder of the changes she was struggling with in her body. Her emotions were muddled: she identified a weak-looking part of her body with a sexual part of herself.

Occasionally when adolescents are afraid of their burgeoning sexuality displayed by body changes, they may react against the changes by trying to appear androgynous in the way they dress. In addition, some adolescent girls may try to diet so that they lose their new womanly shape and even interrupt the menstrual cycle, while others will try to hide behind their fat and use fat to disguise their shape. If an adolescent is deeply pained by an event they may well try to shield themselves behind a metaphorical wall of fat and parents and teachers should be cognisant of this phenomenon.

Mothers, or significant adults, need to talk about menstruation with their daughters so that it is neither a frightening phenomenon nor an excuse for not being competent. Understanding the hormonal fluctuations that occur in their bodies helps girls understand themselves more deeply. Research suggests that the onset of menstruation is associated with a profound change both in the mental representation of the adolescent girl's body and in her self-representation. The onset of menstruation is associated with the first stirring of sexual feeling and with this comes the anxieties of trying to make sense of the new developing adult within.

In cases where there is a distorted understanding of the body, it is imperative that professional help is sought so that the adolescent can come to terms with their wonderful, exciting sexual selves and not shy away from them.

While we have focused on negative plastic surgery, it is important to note that there are instances where plastic surgery can make a valuable contribution towards assisting the adolescent integrate with their new adult body. If there is a marked defect (such as severely protruding ears or an unsightly birthmark) and if a procedure has been carefully thought through with the parents, plastic surgery may create new worlds for an adolescent struggling with a defect.

Other methods of altering the body include the use of make-up and body modification such as piercing and tattooing. Make-up and clothing can serve as a window into the adolescent's internal world. Make-up is a way for adolescents to express their imagination, desires, conflicts and fears. Fatima, in Case Study 27, acknowledged the vulnerability caused by her spotty face. Even if she did not have pimples, like most girls her age she probably would have enjoyed the magical experience of enhancing her appearance by experimenting with make-up.

As adolescents develop a stronger sense of identity, so their make-up and clothing may change. If an adolescent girl's vulnerability is heightened by an event, for example, attending a party, she may apply more make-up or wear clothes that she perceives as hiding her more 'vulnerable shell'. As adolescents become more comfortable with themselves, they tend to be more consistent in how they dress and they tend to develop and feel comfortable with their own style. As they get older, adolescents may be less obsessed with designer labels since they do not need labels to determine their own identities. Invariably older adolescent girls who have integrated various aspects of themselves healthily wear less make-up than those whose personalities are more fluid and who are feeling less secure in themselves.

Body modifications, such as getting a tattoo or having piercings, may have many meanings for an adolescent. Parents could try to understand whether it is the symbol that is tattooed on the adolescent's skin that is important or the painful process in order to get it. The latter reason, as in the case of Sizwe, involves some form of aggression or anger. The adolescent may have chosen to alter or decorate a part of the body that has significance for them. The permanence, if relevant, of the body modification needs to be made clear to the adolescent because they have a tendency to be impulsive and to act rather than think through ideas. There is much debate around body modifications and many argue that tattoos and piercing are simply fashion statements. Body modification usually results from acting out on a fantasy, or it may reflect another deep-seated need.

In our lookist, conformist society in which prejudices are formed on the grounds of appearance, it is becoming increasingly difficult to teach our adolescents to appreciate health and to have an emotionally healthy respect and pride in the body that they have been given. It is no easy task for the parent to assist their adolescent to come to terms with and accept the value of the bodies they have inherited. It is an indictment on our society that while some are starving because of lack of food, others are starving themselves deliberately. How wonderful it would be if we could be a society that truly celebrates difference in all its forms, including body shape.

SUMMING UP

- In adolescence the body changes into a sexual body and boys and girls develop into men and women. This phenomenon can cause complications in the home.

- Adolescents have adult bodies but adolescent minds. As a parent, do not be fooled by their bodies.

- Plastic surgery is not a decision for an adolescent to make; parents must engage with their adolescent should they wish to alter something about their body surgically.

- Be gentle and sensitive to your adolescent's changing shape and guard your comments.

10

October

WHEN THE PARENT COUPLE IS IN TROUBLE

Couples are subjected to many strains and stresses and whether the couple separates or remains together, it is important that they are united in their parenting. This chapter encourages parents to realise that they have responsibilities to parent their adolescents and set boundaries even when they are having relationship difficulties, since sound parenting provides the necessary stability for healthy adolescent development.

OCTOBER IN JOHANNESBURG IS dramatic as electric thunderstorms herald the fact that summer has arrived. After the dry highveld winter, the earth is desperate for the rain and by afternoon the clouds build up in ominously threatening tones of grey. The storms are cathartic and the earth welcomes the potential for growth that the rain clouds portend. Likewise, adolescents would rather the storms in their home could break so that growth and newness could result; rumblings are often far more threatening than realities.

CASE STUDY 29: THE LOSS OF THE FAMILY UNIT AND THE GAINING OF STEP-RELATIONSHIPS

In the third term, Tracy, in Grade 10, is approached by the school chaplain, who has noticed her frowning frequently during various chapel services. The chaplain wants to check if there is anything about the services that is upsetting her. Tracy explains that it has nothing to do with the services, although attending church has triggered some confusing emotions arising from rumblings at home.

Tracy tells her story. She lives with her mother, younger sister, stepfather and older stepsister. She spends every Wednesday and alternate weekend with her father, his girlfriend and her biological sister. Her parents have been divorced for four years. Tracy feels frustrated about many things in the new family set-up, although she acknowledges it is much better than when she lived with her original family.

Tracy is having difficulty with both her parents acting like adolescents at times. She cannot share her annoyance about the one to the other, as 'daggers come out'. Tracy feels sad that she can no longer be spontaneous in her thoughts in relation to her parents. She wishes that 'they would just act like adults and stop trying to compete with each other.' Because she feels that she is an intelligent, thinking adolescent, Tracy says she can see which parent is responsible for which reaction or event and their trying to make out that the other is the villain annoys her. Tracy acknowledges, however, that they are excellent at keeping the boundaries of what she is and is not allowed to do. Although she is annoyed with her parents, Tracy feels safe with them.

When asked what annoys her most, she explains that she gets frustrated with her parents always bickering about finances and that she does not want to know about their concerns and responsibilities. Further, she says that she really does not appreciate her stepfather making assumptions that she and he are close. Tracy says that he is not a father-figure for her; he is simply Mike, her mother's husband. Tracy wishes her mother and stepfather would acknowledge that there is a history to their new family and that there will be differences and different intimacies. They need to understand that she has gone from being the eldest to being the middle child. She wishes they would understand that developing a *real* relationship is more important than trying to play at the *role* of a sister or father.

Tracy confesses she feels a lot better now that she has expressed her thoughts to the chaplain, since it gives her space to acknowledge that she prefers the present situation to the conflict her parents had when they were married. She explains that since becoming an adolescent, she has found it easier to have a more adultlike relationship with her parents and this has given her space to remember that they are also human and will make mistakes.

CASE STUDY 30: WHEN PARENTS HATE EACH OTHER

Normally a bright, achieving student, Jacob's Grade 11 marks are slipping and his hair has started to creep rebelliously over his collar. He is regularly absent from school and he is dismissive of any talk of good relationships in life orientation classes. The life orientation teacher notices his discontent and offers his time to chat if Jacob ever feels the inclination.

About four months down the line, Jacob approaches the teacher and takes up his offer to talk. He confides his disappointment in his parents' relationship and that his experience of their conflict is spilling into his experience at school. He explains that his parents never talk to each other at home and the obvious hatred between them is icy and intense. Jacob explains that he desperately wishes they would go for help because the atmosphere at home is unbearable in its heaviness.

Jacob recounts how his mother has had an affair and his father has caught her out. He feels furious with his mother, and yet understands her actions on one level because his father is sometimes cold and distant. His guess is that his father has issues around intimacy and needs to talk to someone. It has got to the stage where they talk to each other through their children. Jacob also says his younger sister is getting away with murder and engaging in inappropriate sexual encounters. He feels as if his mother and sister always have secrets in an attempt to exclude and shun the father. The mother allows his sister out late at night and Jacob feels that his sister is living a lie in her relationship with their father.

School and his friends are Jacob's only solace. When the teacher asks if he has approached his parents about his concerns, Jacob says he has tried but both parents cut him off saying that he was out of line to speak to them in such a rude way. Jacob had backed down because their rage was incredibly frightening. He has seen objects being smashed at home and he confesses that the thought of his mother or father having a live-in lover is quite upsetting; it is hard for him to determine which situation would be better. Displaying great maturity, Jacob feels that the best option would be for them all to talk to somebody so that they could stop living with hatred attendant at every meal and in every interaction in the home.

DEVELOPMENTAL CONSIDERATIONS AND SUGGESTIONS

Hopefully most infants are born out of love between the parents, who have hopes and dreams of being able to provide a loving family for the infant, to eventually grow old together and to share their love of the adult children. Sadly, the divorce statistics show us that many of these initial dreams do not materialise. Parents may fall out of love for many reasons and if after significant attempts they fail to be reunited, divorce becomes an option. Some couples decide to remain in the relationship, often for the sake of finances or the children, and they may develop meaningful relationships with other adults. The problem arises when the family home becomes emotionally toxic and all the individuals in the family are at great risk of long-term pain and illness, be it physical or emotional.

A family that is separated brings with it losses and gains, but where parents – be they separated or within a relationship – are in conflict, a great deal of damage can occur.

Adolescents from divorced families, or from families where parents do not send a united signal in their parenting, experience less protection than their peers. Although hardships may arise initially when parents part, it does not mean that these difficulties have to continue when the new family situation settles. For example, a couple united in their parenting will offer firm and clear boundaries, making it difficult for the adolescent to slip through the 'cracks' that arise from differences between parents. In the short term adolescents usually love these 'cracks', but when adolescents realise they are being neglected and that they are not being appropriately guided in life, they long for united parents to guide them and to be their source of authority. Watchfulness over adolescents makes them feel loved and important.

In Case Study 29, Tracy did not experience a dissonance in authority or an inconsistency in parenting when her parents separated, since her parents managed to set clear and consistent boundaries despite being in conflict with each other. In other words, Tracy's parents behaved maturely towards their parenting responsibilities because they separated their personal conflict from their parental duty. In addition, their maturity allowed Tracy to come to terms with and articulate her emotions around the divorce.

However, a negative aspect of Tracy's parents' relationship was that they were in competition with each other, an aspect which all separated parents need to guard against carefully. Little children may be fooled by the competition, but adolescents see quite clearly what games may be being played by parents to gain favour with the child or indirectly to send a message to the other parent. Parents who engage in competitive behaviour with each other reduce the sense of self-worth in their child because they have used the child as a battleground for their own ends rather than treating them with the love and respect that good parenting demands. Couples who divorce but respect and love their children in spite of the divorce have understood that they have divorced each other and not their children. Very satisfactory adolescent development can occur when couples keep their divorce difficulties separate from their children.

In Case Study 30 Jacob complained that his sister was getting into trouble and he had started to parent her. Placing older siblings into a parenting role for an extended period of time is selfish and unacceptable behaviour on the part of the parent. If parents are blinded by conflict, adolescents can become neglected because boundaries are often poorly enforced. In addition, their adolescent development is compromised because they have to grow up too quickly, at the expense of their younger needs. Alternatively, if the adolescent feels compromised by the conflict or is pushed into responsibilities they do not want, they may regress and 'act out' in order to be parented and looked after.

When the adolescent has to live between two homes with two sets of rules it is important that the separated parents respect the different rules without trying to change them to be in perfect alignment with their own rules. In other words, one parent should not demand that the same rules apply in both homes if the rules do not significantly affect the safety, health and overall well-being of the adolescent. Nit-picking over rules can be detrimental to the adolescents' relationship with both parents. Separated parents, and indeed all parents, should be careful to provide appropriate boundaries for their adolescents.

There is more acting out among adolescents who live in homes where couples are in extreme conflict than among those in the homes of couples who are consistent in and committed to their parenting. Adolescents tend to be more promiscuous when not guided by their parents. When spoken to, Jacob's sister explained that she was driven by a wish to be held by a man and to be sought after. She rarely saw her father and when she did he seemed to be in a bad mood and unapproachable. Sexual encounters on their own were not her desire but rather the price she was prepared to pay for the attention, albeit short-lived, from a man.

Conversely, adolescents who have reasonable curfews during their high school years seem to postpone sex until their late teens or early twenties, with most having sex only within the context of an established relationship. Although adolescents may not say so directly, they desire and need their parents to have reasonable, consistent rules and to provide supervision. Regardless of whether you are divorced, single or have a live-in lover, the importance of being a *consistent* parent is important. As explained in the Introduction, parents need to be someone the adolescent can lean on for support. If adolescents are not supported, they grow up too quickly and have to create their own boundaries. Alternatively the adolescent continues existing in the parents' boundaryless state and becomes prone to risk-taking behaviour.

Some parents are so overwhelmed by the conflict that ensues from separation that they take out their frustration on their adolescents by creating a home environment that is too rigid, too strict and unsympathetic to the developing adolescent. Parents cannot expect their adolescents to be sympathetic to their conflict-ridden relationships. Parents are the adults and it is their responsibility to be there for the adolescent. Too often the parents in their grief forget their responsibility and mistakenly think that their adolescent is being selfish or unthoughtful.

In order for trust to exist in a home, especially when it has been broken by divorce, it is important for parents to create a trusting environment. Secrets should therefore be kept to a minimum.

Often with divorce and the subsequent relationships that may result, step-parenting may become necessary. It will often be easier to be a step-parent to a young child than to an adolescent, because the parent will have a longer time to build a meaningful relationship with the child. With an adolescent who is developmentally in the process of separating from their parents, developing a deep bond may require more thought and effort. Consider the reality of the adolescent's relationship to both their parents and respect the meaning it has for them. For example, if Tracy was known to have a special bond with her biological father, she should have been helped to look after it, especially because she would see him less often in the new family structure. Younger children can sometimes idealise the parent who is less visible. Adolescents, especially older adolescents, seem to be more able to hold both parents in mind simultaneously. Step-parents need to be mindful of the feelings of adolescents and should allow them to guide the relationship.

It is becoming more common for adults and couples to seek help with their relationship conflict. Adolescents welcome parents' seeking help because they feel safer when the parents are seen to be trying to be in healthy control of themselves and the family.

Relationships can be very hard work and the hard work is continuous. However, the meaning, joy and support that adults, children and adolescents gain from them is immeasurable.

SUMMING UP

- Remain adult when your adolescent talks to you about your relationship.

- Try to acknowledge the mistakes you have made in the marital relationship. Your adolescent will hold you in high regard for it. For adolescents, it is often more about being honest than being right.

- Be patient in developing new step-relationships and do not demand that your adolescent be sympathetic to the new structure. Remember you created it, not your adolescent.

- If the marital relationship is not a loving one, consider getting help to resolve the difficulty for your own sake and that of all the members in the family.

- Parents who remain together but who do not parent together can put their adolescent at risk of feeling insecure.

NOVEMBER

COMMONLY ASKED QUESTIONS AND SOME ANSWERS

Parents have many questions and it is impossible to answer them all. This chapter looks at questions that are frequently asked and attempts to answer them. There are no quick-fix answers, no three easy steps to raising adolescents. We hope other people's questions help you find some answers to your own.

NOVEMBER IS JOYFUL. THE land is abuzz with summer sounds and birdcalls. The lushness of summer gardens calls us to celebrate life and particularly the life that is so abundant in our adolescents. For adolescents, holidays are around the corner, with just a few exams to overcome. Frequent showers cool the earth and everything seems settled and alive. End-of-year parties call us to put on our dancing shoes and be happy.

Do I always have to like my adolescent?

As your adolescent moves towards adulthood it will be impossible to like every aspect of the person. It is more normal to dislike some or other aspect that they have acquired on their journey to adulthood than to be blindly adoring of your adolescent. Invariably you will always *love* your children while not *liking* every aspect of them. Remember that part of an adolescent's getting to know and understand their identity is for them to be able to evoke a range of feelings, including dislike, in you, the parent.

Should I allow my adolescent to date?

Dating that takes place within the context of the family's values is usually a positive place for the adolescent to learn.

If your adolescent has displayed elements of responsibility appropriate to their age, allowing them to date can help them move towards adulthood. Dating can help them learn about love, relationships and themselves within the context of a relationship. The task of adolescence is to move effectively towards being an integrated, responsible adult. Adolescents can only be effective in that move if they begin to separate from their parents and create their own identity. They need their parents' support and supervision throughout the process of moving away, and dating is no different. Because they are not yet adult, the adolescent cannot cope with a completely separate relationship and will need the guidance of a thoughtful parent.

Denying the adolescent the opportunity to date could drive them towards destructive 'acting out' behaviour (discussed in Chapter 5). If they feel mistrusted they may well behave in an untrustworthy manner and may hide relationships from their parents.

Young love is special and exciting and parents can enjoy this time with their adolescents. It need not be fraught with difficulty or hardship.

Until what time should we allow our adolescents to stay out at the weekend?

As a general rule of thumb, 11 o'clock at night is an appropriate time. If there is a specific function that requires a later curfew, this should be carefully negotiated between the adolescent and parents. It may be useful to negotiate a slightly later time for those in Grade 12. If you know your adolescent struggles when they have not had sufficient sleep, this should be brought into the negotiating space; the converse is also applicable. Excessively late nights out are unacceptable.

Should I allow my adolescent to go to clubs? Is it all right to allow them to drink alcohol before they are 18?

This question will be answered by the value system to which the individual family aspires. However, the answer is neither moral nor ethical nor religious; it is far more simple. The law of the country forbids drinking under the age of 18 when parents of the minor are not present. In addition, it is a criminal offence to serve or sell alcohol to a person under the age of 18. Therefore the answer is clear. If you despise corruption and you condemn the lawlessness that sometimes abounds, it is important to abide by the law when it comes to your adolescent. It is important to model appropriate behaviour. In fact the parent has no decision to make in this regard because the law is clear.

Where the law is not prescriptive about the consumption of alcohol is when parents are present with their children and here parents will have to make a decision which supports their family ethos. Parents would do well to remember not only the physiological effects of alcohol on a still-developing brain but also the emotional turmoil that arises from a young person being intoxicated and out of control. If your adolescent is often drunk or you hear reports of drunken behaviour, it is important to ask why your adolescent is trying to dissociate from the world. Too many adolescents are drinking to numb their pain and they need help.

Most clubs have a 'No under-18s policy'. The adolescent in a phase of acting out will want to attend an over-18s club because they think it makes them appear more adult and grown up. Many will beg their parents to help them get a false identity document or they will go behind their parents' backs to acquire a 'fake ID'. Parents who support this criminal behaviour in their adolescents are setting a poor example and are in fact condoning illegal behaviour. Adolescents want to be gratified instantly and they may feel that the wait to turning 18 is interminable but dealing with both waiting and disappointment are essential life skills.

The authors have no shortage of sensational and horrific stories of both male and female adolescents who have been abused or raped or beaten at clubs. Many have had their drinks spiked, with dire consequences. We have tried not to be sensational in this book. Under-aged adolescents who have tried to make themselves look older are easily identifiable and become prey for less scrupulous adults who feel that the very presence of these adolescents gives them licence to do with them as they please. Many parents will argue that equally horrific things will happen at house parties, and in some cases they are right, but invariably many of the adolescents at house parties are known to each other, are of a similar age and there is a modicum of control as a result. Parents should check whether the host parents will be present at adolescent house parties. Parties where there is no adult supervision can be very dangerous.

Parents who serve alcohol to children under the age of 18 at house parties are in fact breaking the law. It will be an interesting case when a parent chooses to sue another parent for breaking the law by serving alcohol to their teenagers under the age of 18. It could be argued that to serve alcohol to a minor endangers their life.

There are also pseudo-clubs; often these are attached to sports clubs. While these pseudo-clubs sometimes have no age restriction, they rarely bother to check the age of the person to whom they are serving alcohol. Drinking contests amongst school-going students at these venues are known to take place and some have even had consenting adults in attendance. The popularity of these pseudo-clubs is related to the fact that they sell alcohol more cheaply than 'real' clubs and so the consumption of alcohol is often greater than at other clubs. Should you agree to allow your child to attend a pseudo-club it is wise to be the parent who both drops and fetches your adolescent to ensure that they have not over-indulged and to ensure that they are safe. We would advise the same strategy for house parties. This may curtail the parents' own social life from time to time but the investment in the future of your adolescent is worth the sacrifice.

Remember the fluid personality of an adolescent requires boundaries. Help your adolescent understand why they really want to go to a club and encourage them to wait for the appropriate time – when they have the physiological and emotional resources to enjoy the experience and cope with any difficulties that may arise. It is important that adolescents have fun, go to parties, socialise and enjoy themselves, but this should be done within the parameters of the law and in a way that helps them move towards being healthy, well-integrated adults in society.

We have tried to treat our son and daughter similarly but our son has more confidence than our daughter – what did we do wrong?

This question speaks to a societal issue rather than an issue in the home and requires a book in itself. Research suggests that girls, more than boys, manifest a 'dysynchrony' in the progression from latency (about age six to nine) to adolescence. Dysynchrony suggests a dissonance between their ability and their *perception* of that ability. Girls tend to see themselves as less than they are, whereas boys can be almost boastful about their ability. Females tend to develop their identity as they experience themselves through attachments in relationships. Given that these relationships are often volatile and fragile, their sense of self and their confidence can be impaired for a time.

The media does little to help girls feel good about themselves and they have to work hard to rise above subliminal messages that are sent.

It is a daunting but rewarding task to raise a confident young woman who believes in herself. Your daughter will grow in confidence as she progresses towards adulthood if you are consistently interested in her and her opinions and who she is. Both boys and girls, but more so girls, will require constant affirmation of your belief in them. Boys are more sensitive than generally thought and need to be allowed to express a wide range of feelings and emotions.

At what age should I let my adolescent use Mxit and other social networking tools?

The answer lies not so much in the chronological age of the adolescent, but rather in the levels of responsibility they display as an individual. Guidelines around technology need to be set by the family in keeping with their family values. To deny your adolescent access to modern technology is to render them inappropriately prepared for modern demands around communication.

It is important that adolescents have clear and reasonable rules around technology and that they have been taught appropriate manners around the use of mobile phones. It may be useful to establish the amount of screen time allowed. Screen time refers to time spent at the computer, in front of television and on the cellphone. The hard task is for parents to adhere to the boundaries they have set.

Should I read my adolescent's text messages or journals?

Generally a parent should obey common rules of decency and privacy, and reading journals is a terrible breach of trust. If your adolescent is trustworthy and responsible, build on these traits. Remember adolescents are extremely sensitive around owning what they have written. If you walk alongside your adolescent consistently, they will invariably share any problematic text messaging with you. If you have shown that you respect their personal space, they are likely to trust you.

If, however, your adolescent has engaged in irresponsible behaviour around the use of technology, you may well have cause to invade their privacy for a period of time or to bar them from the use of technology for a reasonably considered period set down and adhered to by you, the parent.

Sending messages to your adolescent's peers via text messaging or Facebook disempowers your adolescent, particularly in the eyes of their peers.

If you feel compelled to read the private writing of your adolescent or if you go through their private things, you have not allowed the separation process to progress appropriately. Unless you suspect your adolescent of abusing substances or other aberrant behaviour, it is best to respect their private space; they need it.

My adolescent organises everything at the last minute. Arrangements are made via cellphone and everything seems chaotic. How do I get my adolescent to be more organised and not use the cellphone to confirm arrangements just before they are about to happen?

This observation marks the shift parents have to make as they parent in the twenty-first century. Adolescents do not have to make clear meeting points or exact arrangements since their arrangements and plans can be confirmed on Facebook or via text messaging. It can be highly annoying for the controlling and in-control parent. The positive side to remember is that you can locate your child more easily and contact them when they are out.

It may be helpful to think about who the problem of the 'last-minute adolescent organiser' has most affected. If the parent just finds it annoying but it is not significantly affecting their management of their daily life, then the space needs to be negotiated. Tell your adolescent that if you are required to do lifts, for instance, you may insist on more firm arrangements. Not telling you in sufficient time and if it puts your arrangements out considerably – especially when they had a choice to inform you – means the adolescent will forfeit the opportunity of your support. Sitting with the consequence of missing a function, the adolescent should learn to negotiate more time-consciously.

If you see that your adolescent's needs and life in general are suffering because of not thinking ahead enough, it may mean more is required than pointing out choices and consequences in life. Perhaps your adolescent would benefit from some organisational tools or methods that you as parents have adopted to achieve the most out of a day while still feeling comfortably paced. Severe disorganisation or distractibility may require more careful thought as to the origin – for example, neurological or emotional sources – and if this is the case, seeing the appropriate professionals is indicated.

What are appropriate punishments?

Parents make a rod for their backs if they punish too often and are too rule-bound, but they will also cause enormous difficulties if they do not set boundaries. Trying to find the balance is the key to successful, fair, logical and appropriate discipline. Punishment should always fit the misdemeanour. As much as parents may feel like grounding their adolescents until they are 42, parents must try to set punishments that they can adhere to so that they be effective in moving the adolescent towards a healthy adulthood. If punishment is fair and consistent, adolescents will respect the boundary that has been set in place.

Adolescents who have erred sometimes feel better if they are in fact punished so that the offence can be dealt with and then forgotten.

Removal of privileges such as mobile phones and television for short periods of time is usually an effective form of punishment, as is a reasonably thought through period of grounding. Punishment must have a logical link to the misdemeanour and the severity of the punishment should be relevant and neither too punitive nor too lax.

If an adolescent abuses technology, for example, access to technology should be curtailed (within reason, of course, since some schools require students to do research and type up their assignments; you do not want to give your adolescent an excuse not to do their homework). Failure to do homework or to prepare adequately for a test may indicate that too much time has been spent in front of a screen and one or other screen could be denied for a week or so.

Grounding (for a limited time) can be used when adolescents have been excessively rude, misused time or broken trust. If an adolescent fails or forgets to complete a chore, it may be useful to ask them to forfeit something they enjoy in return for the forgotten chore. Piling on additional chores may result in the adolescent feeling overwhelmed.

Try to adhere to punishments set and try not to set them too harshly so that in a kinder moment you feel compelled to relent and thus appear weak and malleable for future confrontations. Also, it is important to find your adolescent doing some things well so that you can praise and acknowledge their triumphs more frequently than you punish them.

If the misbehaviour is – or borders on – very serious and criminal, seek professional help immediately.

Always try to separate the misdemeanour from the individual by criticising the behaviour rather than the person. This is easier said than done. Avoid words like 'always' and 'never' and if you overreact, apologising will go a long way to appeasing your adolescent, so long as it is not repeated 'acting out' behaviour on the part of the parent.

How do I relate to my adolescent who is so changeable – five years old one day and 25 the next?

When your adolescent acts like a five year old, understand that they are feeling vulnerable and out of control. They need to be contained, held and understood, not humiliated for reverting to childlike behaviour. Try to understand the source of the behaviour and why they are feeling insecure. When they are acting beyond their years, they are practising new beliefs. Acknowledge the worth that you find in the behaviour while gently feeding back any incongruous behaviour. Remember too that young adolescents tend to display more erratic behaviour than older adolescents whose personalities and identities are becoming less fluid than their young counterparts.

How do I help my child respond to criticism from another adult or teacher?

First acknowledge the pain your adolescent will feel. Try not to add your criticism to that of the criticism received. Then try to separate the message from the delivery if the latter has been harsh. If there was value in the message, try to integrate that while discarding any unkindness that may have attended the criticism and which in fact belongs to the messenger. Try to teach your child to welcome criticism rather than to fear it, since this will make them stronger adults. If you can teach your adolescent to embrace criticism and see the merit in it, you will have been an excellent parent. It may also help to discuss defence mechanisms and how criticism is hurtful at first but may be useful once it has been heard and understood. However, cruelty and bullying tactics are not helpful and should not be condoned since these can be very destructive to a burgeoning identity.

When and how should I approach the school if I have a problem?

If your adolescent is regularly unhappy or is struggling academically, you should ask the school for help. If something traumatic has happened at home – from crime through to a death in the family – you should inform the school. A pet dying can have an impact on an adolescent's learning. A simple call to the school to let them know what has happened helps the school manage your adolescent better. If your adolescent has a teacher who is a bully you must approach the school, and if you think your adolescent is being bullied or is a bully you should inform the school of your concerns. Any inkling of abuse must be reported to the school. If one of the parents is seriously ill, the school should be informed so that they can best care for the adolescent.

It is courtesy to call the school to let them know if your child is away from school for any reason. Having basic good manners in your interactions with the school will mean that it is easier to approach the school if and when there is a more serious problem.

If at all possible encourage your adolescent to address the problem before stepping in if the issue pertains to them specifically. If you have a problem that is not appropriate for your adolescent to attempt to solve, try to find a teacher you trust and ask them for guidance if you do not want to go to the head teacher immediately. If your adolescent has a problem with a teacher, try to address it directly with that teacher first; failing which you may have to escalate the complaint.

Schools welcome constructive criticism and they resent serial complainers. Schools tend to react negatively to confrontations and threats but good schools will always be happy to listen to concerns of parents in an attempt to make their schools better places of learning. Remember there are always many sides to a problem so try not to be overly angry when approaching the school. Try to make appointments rather than barging in unannounced.

Remember it is your right to approach the school respectfully. Before you go, remember the three questions raised earlier in the book:

1. Is the problem a result of an inherent shortcoming in my child that I need help to manage?
2. Is the problem in fact my issue as a parent, which I have not fully resolved in myself?
3. Has the school misunderstood my child?

If you accidentally overreact, do not hesitate to apologise since it is the adult thing to do. If the school has made a mistake, allow them the opportunity to apologise and make amends.

Avoid seeking advice from other parents, who are invariably ill-informed, and at all costs try to avoid being the school gossip. Schools are well aware of which parents malign them and you lose credibility as a parent in the eyes of your adolescent if you regularly do this. Your adolescent needs to respect their place of learning and if you as a parent always undermine the school, your adolescent will feel disconnected from school.

Avoid going to the press or taking legal action unless your child has been harmed through negligence. Seek mediation before litigation. The consequences for the adolescent whose name appears in the press can be dire.

Schools are responsible places and they are responsible for the well-being of the adolescents in their care. If you are in doubt about approaching the school, err on the side of caution and approach the school rather than regretting not having done so when a problem becomes unmanageable.

What do I do if my adolescent does not receive an award I know is deserved?

First of all ask yourself how you know that your adolescent deserves the award and review the awards criteria every school should have. Remember it is hard for you to know every other student's capabilities in comparison to those of your child. If you genuinely feel that your adolescent has been mistreated or overlooked, you will have to approach the school. Remember, if you ask the question, be prepared for the answer. Sometimes awards are held back on account of poor behaviour and you will be required to respect the boundaries set down by the school.

If possible, and for the purposes of increasing development and awareness, encourage your adolescent to approach the relevant teacher or even the head of the school to query the perceived oversight. Sometimes your adolescent has been accidentally overlooked and the school will need to have the error pointed out. Mistakes happen; allow the school to make amends. Schools sometimes make mistakes and are unable to acknowledge them – this is hard work and you will have to help your adolescent process the reality that unfair things happen in life. Unprofessional teachers will hide their dislike of a student behind all kinds of excuses and make dishonest choices around that adolescent. This happens and it is often difficult to prove. Allow your child to work through the disappointment and to accept that there are those who are too small-minded to enjoy the success of others. At other times your adolescent may not have met the mark and you will have to help them process the disappointment. It is perfectly acceptable and normal to feel disappointment but this should never be allowed to become so big that it is a deterrent for future success.

Awards should not be the only reason to try for excellence. We need to teach our adolescents that the process is sometimes more important than the prize.

How do I understand the academic ability of my adolescent?

Try to review your adolescent as a complete person rather than as a series of comments and numbers on a school report. Consider how your adolescent interacts with adults and peers and how they manage the various aspects of their lives. Think about how they interpret and respond to broader social issues, whether their thinking is sophisticated or very concrete and whether their number ability and linguistic skills are competent. Once you have considered these things carefully you should be able to make an assessment of your adolescent's ability, but if you remain unsure you can engage the services of diagnosticians skilled in assessing the aptitude of adolescents. Remember however that the brain is still developing during adolescence. Professional career guidance conducted by specialist psychologists at about Grade 11 can be very useful.

Schools are places of teaching and learning. Do not expect them to do everything from career selection to identifying psychological problems.

Should I give my adolescent pocket money and should it be linked to doing chores in the house?

Pocket money managed sensibly is an ideal way to teach your adolescent budgeting skills. It is a good idea to give an adolescent pocket money that encourages an awareness of financial constraints and the need to budget. It is not wise to give your adolescent too much pocket money, no matter how wealthy the parent is. Negotiate which expenses you will cover and which things you expect your adolescent to pay for from the allowance. Entertainment, gifts for friends and casual clothing are areas for which your adolescent could be responsible. Doing chores in the home need not be attached to pocket money. Chores, which are not onerous and which are reduced at times of stress such as during exams, help an adolescent feel integrated and part of a community outside of themselves. Chores can develop a deeper sense of responsibility and of worthwhile contribution. However, avoid making chores an area of conflict and try not to conflate chores and punishment.

What do I do if one of the friends in my adolescent's peer group engages in risky behaviour?

If you are completely certain that the friend is involved in something dangerous, it is your responsibility to alert the parents of the friend. You should refrain from telling the school or making it a point of discussion amongst your adult peers. Be aware that the news will not be met with great enthusiasm and you may have a very angry situation to manage. Some immature adults may ostracise you for having taken a stand, while others may be very grateful for your courage. Your own adolescent may resent your intervention and it is therefore important to be sure of the facts. If you are worried about the fallout of your actions in protecting a young person and your adolescent asks you not to be involved, it is perhaps worth thinking about the maxim: 'Better an angry friend than a dead friend.'

If you do not have concrete evidence and what you hear is speculation and rumour, desist from perpetuating the stories. Also ask yourself what you would like to know if it were your adolescent. Think about how you would like to be told if your adolescent were involved in risk-taking behaviour, such as excessive alcohol consumption. If someone approaches you about your adolescent's behaviour, consider what is being said carefully and help your adolescent. Unfortunately there are always mischief-makers and it is important to ensure the veracity of any comments before taking drastic action. Keep an open mind and try to understand that the information is intended to help. If the person is a typical gossip then treat the information sceptically, but remember there might be some truth around the allegations.

As adults we are obliged to help all young people flourish.

Is community service really important? Schools tend to put so much emphasis on it and it is so time-consuming.

Irrespective of schools insisting on community service, developing an awareness of the broader community within the family context is enriching. The family can experience many things through serving the community charitably. It is a wonderful source of developing self-esteem and purpose in a young person's life and it can also be a bonding time for families. In addition, involvement in community service can create a special place for struggling adolescents to find a niche.

My son is an avid sportsman and is talented but he is smaller than his peers and insists on drinking protein shakes. Is this acceptable?

Employing the advice of an ethical doctor who can provide appropriate dietary advice to build muscles is the best solution. Excessive gyming and concern with body image in boys and girls is unhealthy and needs to be managed. The taking of steroids is extremely dangerous and should be strongly discouraged.

I feel like an ATM machine with taxi capabilities. How do I stop resenting this?

As in infancy, accept that your adolescent needs you. Try to do things together from time to time that validate your relationship rather than the chores you are obliged to do as a parent. Adolescence passes quickly and you will miss the storms and thunderbolts in your home when it is over. Enjoy your adolescent – an ATM with taxi capabilities is a rather marvellous machine after all!

My adolescent never seems grateful for all I do and sacrifice. How do I make them more grateful?

Understand that adolescence is by necessity a very selfish developmental stage. Deep gratitude may not yet be felt by an adolescent, so their reluctance to say thank you may mean that they have not yet reached that developmental milestone. Many will say thank you out of habit and politeness rather than genuine feeling. It is your duty and responsibility to provide basic necessities for your adolescent. If you have pampered and mollycoddled your child since birth it will take some time to realign your family values and you will need to explain what you are doing to your child. Living in a consumerist society where instant gratification has become the norm has made adolescents assume they are entitled to a great deal. It takes a careful and courageous parent to stand against these aberrational values and to allow their adolescent to benefit from the rewards of delayed gratification.

Usually by their late teens and certainly by their early twenties most adolescents tend to show more appreciation for what they have received.

What do I do if my child is exceedingly untidy?

Close their bedroom door. Early adolescents are typically chaotic and disorganised – it is where they are at developmentally. Ongoing untidiness may simply be part of the constitutional make-up of the adolescent, which you have to accommodate. Respect their space but request, firmly, that they respect your space by keeping communal areas tidy. Do not waste precious life fighting this issue.

If, however, you feel that the untidiness is symptomatic of something more serious, then think about what the untidiness means or represents in the adolescent. For example, does the adolescent need general help with organisational skills (in which case developing the tidy room may help them learn the value of order) or is the untidiness representative of identity, creativity, freedom or a busyness that does not afford the adolescent sufficient time to tidy their room effectively?

Does conflict in the home really have an effect on the adolescent?

Conflict between the parenting couple may impede the adolescent's growing up. Typically adolescents will use the issue of couple conflict as a scapegoat for their own difficulties and to push boundaries. They can, when there is parental conflict, split the couple into the favoured and non-favoured parent. Adolescents use splitting as a form of defence and can exploit fundamental differences between parents. If you have been married for a long time, conflicts can sometimes be more overt because there is greater confidence in the relationship and the way in which issues are managed are more entrenched. It is then valuable that as a couple and as a family you consciously review how to support each other. Conflict avoidance can be as detrimental to an adolescent's development as excessive conflict. Teaching adolescents that conflict occurs and can be resolved is affording them another life skill. Violence should never be condoned in any form.

Does crime and living in a violent society affect my child?

Our environment always has an impact on how we feel about the space we are in, whether we are adult or adolescent. If you are involved in an attack and are unsure of your adolescent's response, it may be valuable to seek the guidance of a counsellor. Adolescents can be indirectly traumatised if their peers are harmed or attacked in any way and parents should be sensitive to their fears.

Sleeping is often disturbed by trauma and adolescents may want to return to their parents' bed to feel safe. Empathise with their fear and talk about it but encourage them to return to normality as soon as possible.

What do I do if my adolescent still sleeps in my bed?

If your adolescent is not able to separate from a parent or family, there are a few things to think about. When did the fear of separation or change occur? If the fear has existed since early childhood, the adolescent has struggled with independence (see the Introduction and Chapter 1). Whatever is blocking the independence needs to be dealt with and may require professional help.

Significant anxiety is not to be underestimated in an individual; although it may seem simple to some to sleep alone, extreme anxiety can debilitate an adolescent. Parents can ask themselves whether separating is the child's issue or the parent's issue. For example, perhaps from childhood the adolescent has been reserved in nature and that is their inherent personality. Parents can help bridge the road to independence for a reserved child by showing them the trust that you have that they will in fact be all right and that they have the necessary skills to learn to enjoy being away from parents. If parents recognise that they struggle separating from their adolescent (Chapter 3) for whatever reason, then they need to resolve their own anxiety because it is hindering the adolescent from moving towards maturity. If the reason for an enmeshment between the adolescent and family is because of a past or present trauma, a balance of allowing the adolescent some resting space from that trauma and then guiding them to feel that they can be in control once again is important. Together the adolescent and family must engage in recovery that will assist with a gradual rebuilding of the original confidence that they enjoyed before the traumatic event. Remember after trauma your adolescent will feel more dependent for a while.

An adolescent's bedroom is so valuable in the growing up process. For example, being able to have a bedroom that represents their identity helps them to learn what they like about themselves and what they want to discard. Sometimes this means painting the walls different colours, changing posters, learning whether they are a neat or disorganised individual. Being alone at night also affords the adolescents time to reflect on the day and integrate all the different parts of their life.

Must I always send my adolescent on school outings and camps?

Most school outings and camps play a significant part in the academic and social development of the adolescent and are carefully placed in a school curriculum. Being away from home for a short period of time, even if the circumstances are uncomfortable, is good for an adolescent.

As a general rule it is a worthwhile exercise to send your adolescent on school outings and camps as they serve many purposes in adolescent development, including integration and socialisation. New environments sometimes allow adolescents to discover new things about themselves.

If you fear your adolescent being away from you or your adolescent fears being away from home, then there are more serious issues that need to be addressed therapeutically.

Is there anything I can do to help motivate my adolescent to work at academic endeavours?

As a parent you can help to create an environment conducive to academic endeavour. Your adolescent should have a place where they can work and leave their things. Some adolescents need to spread themselves out when they are studying and may occupy more than one space to do so. During the set homework time or study time it is helpful if parents also engage in quiet activity rather than having the television blaring enticingly. If the home is quiet and studious, then it is easier for adolescents not to be distracted or feel that their work is a punishment since the whole family is quietly engaged in a 'work-related' activity. During examinations it is not wise to organise functions or outings – try to create a studious atmosphere in the home that reflects a learning environment. Do not invite guests around at that time and respect your adolescent's need to apply themselves to the academic demands of school.

Perseverance should be rewarded as much as good marks. Adolescents tend to give up too quickly and do not grapple with issues and problems. Reward the 'grappling process'.

Families who work hard and play hard and who respect the demands on each of the family members are very often successful in many of their endeavours.

Can I change my parenting or mitigate past mistakes?

If you have identified a need to change then you are already halfway through the process towards more consistent parenting. All parents fumble from time to time. Adolescence is a time of enormous change and just when the parent thinks they have understood one aspect of their adolescent, there is something new to manage. Acknowledging significant parenting errors with your adolescent can be helpful in developing a meaningful bond and even allowing your adolescent to see the worth of realigning values. You could work out a new strategy with your adolescent and establish rules that build an effective relationship.

Is boarding school really an option?

Some families may be more independent of each other as part of their family ethos and in this instance boarding school can be an option. Some adolescents may need or want more structure than certain homes offer and again a good boarding school would be a useful consideration. If travelling or distance is problematic or if there is a complicated home situation where there are fraught relationships, boarding school is often a healthy alternative. When relationships are difficult it is sometimes positive to have time apart. This separation needs to be made mindfully and siblings who will be left at home also need to be taken into consideration. Boarding school should never be used as a threat or a punishment.

Be sure to investigate your choice of boarding school carefully.

Certain issues should be considered. For example, who takes care of the children when they are not at school and in the boarding house? Will certain values important to you still be inculcated in your adolescent, for example, will they have a chance to observe religious practices? Will table manners be encouraged? Will there be healthy meal options and is the person looking after your adolescent responsible, mature and psychologically stable? How much is left to prefects and older adolescents? Is the environment nurturing and kind or old-fashioned and oppressive?

If you select the boarding school option, try not to opt out of your adolescent's life completely. They will still need and want you to attend some functions and be interested in them.

How do I get my adolescent to read?

Adolescent and indeed adult reading patterns are often established in infancy. If books are valued in the home and reading encouraged as a worthwhile activity, then reading may be adopted by the adolescent. There are many distractions for twenty-first century adolescents, particularly as a result of advances in technology, and reading time may be compromised. However, by allowing adolescents to purchase and download audiobooks from the internet, for example, they could listen to books on their MP3 players and thus begin to integrate reading and listening into their many activities. Long car journeys can be used for listening to books too and this may encourage adolescents to begin reading. Many adolescents may want to read only non-fiction or vice versa, and their taste in reading material should be respected.

Allow adolescents to choose their own reading material rather than insisting on reading matter you think is relevant or necessary. The recent *Twilight* series has encouraged many adolescents to read. If they are reluctant readers you may also want to consider rewarding them for books read by buying them movie tickets if they have read the book first. Reading must never be seen as a chore. As tempting as it may be, try not to set up television and reading in a contest; see them as mutually exclusive activities.

If your adolescent strongly resists reading and is frustrated by the activity, it is important to ensure that there is no underlying difficulty impairing the process. For example, it is important to have their eyes tested by a specialist optician who is au fait with eye-tracking issues. Other underlying problems may be identified by a trained diagnostician or the adolescent may simply not be prepared to persevere.

Books open many worlds for adolescents so it is sad when they do not read widely.

What is the most important thing I can do for my adolescent?

Be very interested in your adolescent and be excited about the joy of having an adolescent in your home. They are wonderful. Show your interest by attending their sports matches and other events. Praise their achievements but don't demand that they achieve beyond their ability. By criticising the success of their peers you will be inadvertently sending a message of disappointment to your adolescent. Acknowledge not only their successes but validate them as thinking, special human beings. Let them feel that you think they are getting things right more often than not.

Say yes to their requests for lifts more often than you say no. When you say no with a reason and logic, the adolescent is able to understand and accept the negative reply rather than seeing the denying of a request simply as a matter of parental convenience.

Listen meaningfully to their chatter and ask open questions that require them to give in-depth answers. Try to remember what is important to them. Available, listening, boundary-setting and acknowledging parents are 'good enough' parents (a concept explored in the Introduction).

DECEMBER

ENDINGS AND THE IMPORTANCE OF PLAY

Endings are inevitable, much as change is. In this final chapter we look not only at endings but also at the value of laughter and play.

DECEMBER'S WEATHER HAS CELESTIAL overtones. The incredible blueness of the sky, the sounds and scents of summer, lush grass and lazy days can diminish our year-end anxieties. School is over for the year and what has been lost and won can be forgotten for a while at least. It is a time of magic and wonder and play; a time for reflection and hope; and it is a time to express joy deeply. It is a divine time indeed, although endings bring with them both joy and hope for the future and pain at what will be lost.

CASE STUDY 31: AN UNLIKELY TEDDY BEARS' PICNIC

The end of the year is closing in; it is the penultimate day of the school year. There is a sense of excitement for the holidays and a paradoxical sense of both loss and achievement in the air. Exams are over, the drag and joy of results has been dealt with and for the adults it is a time of wrapping up, albeit rather frenetically. The pupils are gathering the debris in their lockers; finding lost socks and belts and ties and trying to stay out of the way of harassed teachers. But the ebullience of December and the end of the term cannot be ignored. There is a sense of something mischievous afoot as pupils walk past the principal's office with an air of furtiveness.

In the frenetic panic of finalising the end of the term, the principal has been rushing in and out of meetings with teachers and parents. The appointment schedule has been back to back; there have been difficult resolutions to discuss before the term ends, but the pupils – ignorant of the demands on the adults – want to celebrate.

On this particularly beautiful December day, the principal rushes into her office after attending a meeting in another part of the school. She is about to start a difficult meeting with a parent, who is already waiting for her. She throws open the door to her office, the angry parent right behind her, and together they step into a completely transformed place. The office has become the idyllic scene of a teddy bears' picnic! Teddy bears are seated on, behind and under the desk. In the meeting area of the office a group of beautiful bears are seated around the table, ready to partake of sumptuous tea and cake. The room with its festive air is a far cry from the serious place it has sometimes had to be during the year.

The principal and the parent look at each other, aghast at first, and then laughter erupts from the depth of the father's belly, completely diffusing the tension. Although he had been irate moments before, he is suddenly overcome by the levity of the situation; he is made aware of joy and life and laughter.

Although the meeting has to be rescheduled to another venue, the tone is probably vastly different from what it would have been and the resolutions taken in it probably far more effective than originally imagined possible.

CASE STUDY 32: PLAYFULLY CELEBRATING THE MOVE TO ADULTHOOD AND A WORLD BEYOND SCHOOL

The last day of their entire school career is drawing closer and the Grade 12 class wants to have some fun. They disguise their excitement and their need to be young and silly by pretending their antics are for the amusement of the younger students in the school. In reality it is not only about their excitement of what is to come, but it is also about their unspoken fears for the future.

As is often the case, many of the matrics' ideas for creating fun are expressed through actions that take them back to their childhood. This particular class has decided that on the last day of school the boys and girls would wear their primary school uniforms. If they do not still have them, they have borrowed diminutive uniforms from acquaintances and relatives. The planning has generated huge hilarity, since it is impossible for most of them to fit into the uniforms. The girls have decided to put their hair in pigtails and some wear little girls' party dresses, if they really could not fit into primary school dresses, while the boys have squeezed themselves into miniscule shorts and shirts that invariably can't be buttoned up. The absurdity of hairy chests and legs emerging from 'little boy' clothes and significant bulges below the waistline is hilarious in its incongruity.

On the final day of school the boys and girls parade through the usually dour school corridors in their zany outfits. The younger students relish the brief disruption from the routine of day-to-day lessons and the hilarity amongst the Grade 12s helps them to realise that not only have they reached the momentous milestone of leaving school but also, more immediately, the holidays are imminent.

Some of the teachers are unimpressed with their ludicrous behaviour, but their disdain only adds to the silliness of the occasion. In any event, most of the pupils are so uncomfortable they soon change back into normal garb once they have enjoyed their display of 'returning to the past'.

CASE STUDY 33: JOY AND PAIN – THE PARADOX OF ENDINGS

Robyn has come into the principal's office to say goodbye and thank you. School has been, by and large, a positive experience for her. She has had good relationships with her teachers and peers, and on account of her excellent academic performance and sporting achievements, she has been awarded a prestigious scholarship.

As she sits in the principal's office both weeping and laughing, she is every bit both lovely young woman and vulnerable girl. The emotions she is feeling are contradictory: incredible excitement for the life waiting for her beyond school, but at the same time a sense of anxiety at having to leave the safety of a school where she has flourished and developed into an exceptional young woman. The awkwardness of adolescence has passed and she is ready for the world, but the pain of saying goodbye is real and cannot be avoided. Even though she wants to move on, she is overwhelmed at the thought of letting go of the deep sense of security she feels in the place and the people. It is at once daunting and exhilarating; sad and wonderful.

The principal lets a tear slip too. Robyn has been exemplary and the school would miss her, even though there are equally talented students to follow in her footsteps. There is always a loss in a goodbye and the change that the ending brings is unavoidable.

A final hug, a swopping of email addresses and promises of continued contact end a poignant but very special farewell.

DEVELOPMENTAL CONSIDERATIONS AND SUGGESTIONS

The conclusion of terms or the school year often offers more time to play. In all likelihood play has been neglected territory for much of the year. Although some of us have forgotten how to, we all like to play. In play we can pretend to be more omniscient and omnipotent than we are in reality; it affords us a momentarily divine and dreamlike space where we do not have constraints.

It can be relaxing to watch children play because they are spontaneous. Adolescents, too, can be so surprising in what they think about and how they play.

Winnicott, the paediatric psychiatrist and psychoanalyst central to the adolescent theory in this book, speaks about the importance of play. He believes that when two or more people are together it usually involves some form of play. The idea of play as a serious and important element in human civilisation is an ancient one. To think about the beginnings of play in a human life, one can go back to the baby and the mother, or primary caregiver. The mother – or caregiver – plays a part for the infant first, as she is in a position to respond spontaneously to the infant's needs. This allows the infant to have an experience of being magical, getting the mother to be and do various things. Winnicott talks about how the confidence in the mother provides an immediate playground for the infant where the idea of magic originates, since the infant experiences feelings of being very strong and able. Sooner or later, the mother introduces her own playing and infants vary in their capacity to like or dislike the introduction of ideas that are not their own. Given the start of the separation process, both mother and child are in a position to play together in a relationship.

As infant and mother experience play, so too do adolescents with their friends and family. Play is immensely exciting, not only because the instincts are involved but also because it allows for other feelings and ideas about the self to be explored. Playing is the precarious interplay between the thoughts and fantasies you have within yourself and the experience of what is actually happening with the person with whom you are playing. Winnicott says, '[Play] is the precariousness of magic itself, magic that arises in intimacy, in a relationship that is found to be reliable' (1971b, p 47). In Case Study 31, that of the teddy bears' picnic, we can see that there the adolescents had the capacity to enjoy other people's reactions to their sense of play. The teddy bears reminded them of their childhood and there was a sense of nostalgia in how they chose to play.

Adolescents who play are encouraging enriching experiences for one another. Playing therefore is not to be confused with 'acting out'. Playing is positive, enjoyable and happy, and the adolescent is creatively alive and part of the present moment. In 'acting out', on the other hand, an adolescent's emotions or feelings are detached from the moment being experienced.

So often adolescents will say they feel so overwhelmed from thinking that they just want to relax and play. Parents are encouraged to give their adolescents a state of 'being in-between the real and inner world', where from 'just being' comes a state of newness. For example, this may involve an adolescent lying on their bed for a while, listening to lyrics on an MP3 player or simply just being. However, numbing their minds with alcohol or zoning out by doing anything excessive, or sleeping with a fatigued head, is not playing. One could consider this induced numbness as a blocking out of emotions or thoughts and interactions with oneself or others. This is not playing, and rather than being potentially creative – as in play – the behaviour is potentially destructive.

Parents who provide opportunities for play also create important memories and events on which their children can build their own ideas and develop self-concepts that are lasting and valuable.

On a practical level, parents can ask themselves whether they are exposing their adolescents to sufficient cultural experiences. Taking them to the theatre, concerts or exhibitions, for instance, could add an element of play that leads to a deeper understanding of the self within the world. By being provided with a variety of opportunities and experiences, particularly in a non-threatening environment, adolescents learn about themselves, the world and what pursuits are worthy of their attention.

In Case Study 33, Robyn acknowledges the joy and the pain inherent in endings. For the adolescent, ending a school year – or finishing school itself – suggests both progress and a growing separate identity. Robyn will be contemplating how she is moving towards becoming a truly separate individual.

Interestingly, endings invite deeper intimacy in relationships with other people. For example, adolescents will leave a school group to be separate individuals when a year ends. It is important that they have therefore developed a capacity to be alone from time to time. This is a very important process, since only when a person has the capacity to be alone do they paradoxically have the capacity to be appropriately intimate in a relationship with another person. This capacity to be both alone and intimate does not develop unless the parents have met their adolescents' needs in a reliable manner during critical phases of separation. In other words, they needed to be 'good enough' parents, the concept explored at the beginning of this book.

Intimacy is a human need, yet many factors inhibit the capacity for intimacy. Ironically the capacity for intimacy develops from the separation process that takes place between the mother and child. It is important therefore that adolescents develop the capacity to cope with endings and do not feel abandoned or devalued by them. Parents need to talk through the meanings of endings with their adolescents. Robyn, although happy, needs to work through all the intricacies of what the ending of school represents. The moving away not only from the security of school but also from the security of her ever-present parents is an important conversation that Robyn could have with her parents. By pre-empting the possible pain in the loss caused by the ending, parents can help adolescents gradually let go and integrate exciting new beginnings into their thinking.

Adolescents may resist dealing with their feelings and assumptions around separation and endings. Throughout adolescence there are many points of ending (and concomitant new beginnings) that mark periods of growth and development.

The act of separation in the form of term endings can be a dynamic creative time for focusing on the adolescent self and understanding that the ending provides an opportunity for growth. Adolescents completing a year of high school can reflect on the things they have learnt and achieved in the year. Teachers will often comment that when adolescents return to school after their holidays, particularly in the Grade 9 and 10 years, they notice a marked growth in maturity. These adolescents have integrated thoughts from previous endings and typically tend to be more grown up than previously. In addition, during holidays adolescents develop in maturity since they develop a growing self-reliance on account of the process of separation from their peers.

Endings can be a time of celebration. Parents can celebrate with their adolescents if goals have been met and tasks accomplished. At the end of each school year parents should try to resolve any complicated issues that have arisen from negative endings so that the next beginning can be positive and valuable. Generally, endings at school should be positive since there should be a validation of work completed and growth accomplished.

Endings cause change, and change is inevitable. So we end our book where we began – change needs to be managed. Endings need to be understood. Both the joy and the inherent loss need to be brought into the open and made real.

The weather and feelings concomitant with December are rich and hopeful; so too are the experiences created by play. Just as play must come to an end and reality accepted, so too must the experiences of the year end. Celebrating what has been learnt and achieved in a year is a form of play and is a means of providing closure to those lessons and achievements, allowing adolescents to face their new opportunities with excitement.

SUMMING UP

- We all like to play. Play reminds us of the importance of sometimes being able to think differently.

- Adults who have forgotten how to play should try to rekindle a sense of fun in their lives.

- Parents can reflect on the space the family has given to play and if there is too much seriousness, they should introduce more play.

- Endings are filled with mixed feelings: sadness at what will be left behind but joy for what is to come.

- Parents should not underestimate the ambivalent feelings that surround endings.

- Healthy endings suggest a time to be alone and an ability to be alone paradoxically creates a platform for more appropriate intimacy in relationships with others.

BIBLIOGRAPHY

Kilborne, B (2002) *Disappearing Persons: Shame and Appearance*, Albany: SUNY Press.

Lorand, S (1961) The body image and the psychiatric evaluation of patients for plastic surgery, *Journal of the Hillside Hospital*, pp 224–32.

Roberts, K (1995) *Youth and Employment in Modern Britain*, London: Oxford University Press.

Simmons, R (2003) *Odd Girl Out: The Hidden Culture of Aggression in Girls*, USA: Harcourt Brace International.

Winnicott, DW (1956) Primary maternal preoccupation, in DW Winnicott (Ed), *Collected Papers: Through Paediatrics to Psychoanalysis*, London: Hogarth Press (1975), pp 300–305.

Winnicott, DW (1958) The capacity to be alone, in DW Winnicott (Ed), *The Maturational Processes and the Facilitating Environment: Studies in the Theory of Emotional Development*, London: Hogarth Press (1965), pp 29–36.

Winnicott, DW (1960a) The relationship of a mother to her baby at the beginning, in DW Winnicott (Ed), *The Family and Individual Development*, London: Tavistock/Routledge (1965), pp 15–20.

Winnicott, DW (1960b) The theory of the parent–infant relationship, in DW Winnicott (Ed), *The Maturational Processes and the Facilitating Environment: Studies in the Theory of Emotional Development*, London: Hogarth Press (1965), pp 37–55.

Winnicott, DW (1960c) Ego distortion in terms of true and false self, in DW Winnicott (Ed), *The Maturational Processes and the Facilitating Environment: Studies in the Theory of Emotional Development*, London: Hogarth Press (1965), pp 140–52.

Winnicott, DW (1961) Adolescence: Struggling through the doldrums, in *The Family and Individual Development*, London: Tavistock/Routledge (1965), pp 79–87.

Winnicott, DW (1962) Ego integration in child development, in DW Winnicott (Ed), *The Maturational Processes and the Facilitating Environment: Studies in the Theory of Emotional Development*, London: Hogarth Press (1965), pp 56–63.

Winnicott, DW (1963a) From dependence toward independence in the development of the individual, in DW Winnicott (Ed), *The Maturational Processes and the Facilitating Environment: Studies in the Theory of Emotional Development*, London: Hogarth Press (1965), pp 83–92.

Winnicott, DW (1963b) Communicating and not communicating leading to a study of certain opposites, in DW Winnicott (Ed), *The Maturational Processes and the Facilitating Environment. Studies in the Theory of Emotional Development*, London: Hogarth Press (1965), pp 179–92.

Winnicott, DW (1963c) Hospital care supplementing intensive psychotherapy in adolescence, in DW Winnicott (Ed), *The Maturational Processes and the Facilitating Environment: Studies in the Theory of Emotional Development*, London: Hogarth Press (1965), pp 242–8.

Winnicott, DW (1964) *The Child, the Family and the Outside World*, Harmondsworth: Penguin.

Winnicott, DW (1965) *The Maturational Processes and the Facilitating Environment: Studies in the Theory of Emotional Development*, London: Hogarth Press.

Winnicott, DW (1967) Mirror-role of mother and family in child development, in P Lomas (Ed), *The Predicament of the Family: a Psycho-analytical Symposium*, London: Hogarth Press.

Winnicott, DW (1971a) Transitional objects and transitional phenomena, in DW Winnicott (Ed), *Playing and Reality*, London: Tavistock/Routledge, pp 1-25.

Winnicott, DW (1971b) *Playing and Reality*, London: Tavistock/ Routledge.

Winnicott, DW (1986) *Home is Where We Start From: Essays by a Psychoanalyst*, New York and London: WW Norton.

Index